Capturing the Power
of Diversity

Capturing the Power of Diversity

Marvin D. Feit, PhD
John H. Ramey, MA, Soc. Admn.
John S. Wodarski, PhD
Aaron R. Mann, PhD
Editors

The Haworth Press
New York • London

The Haworth Press, Inc., 10 Alice Street, Binghamton, NY 13904-1580

Library of Congress Cataloging-in-Publication Data

Symposium on Social Work with Groups (13th : 1991 : Akron, Ohio)
    Capturing the power of diversity : selected proceedings of the XIIIth Symposium on Social Work with Groups, Akron, Ohio, U.S.A., October 31-November 3, 1991 / edited by Marvin D. Feit . . . [et al.].
       p.   cm.
    Includes bibliographical references (p.   ) and index.
    ISBN 1-56024-971-4 (hard)
    1. Social group work–Congresses. 2. Social work with minorities–Congresses. 3. Multiculturalism–Congresses. I. Feit, Marvin D. II. Title.
HV45.S93 1991
351.4–dc20
                                               94-47540
                                                   CIP

CONTENTS

ABOUT THE EDITORS

Marvin D. Feit, PhD, is Professor and Director, School of Social Work, The University of Akron.

John H. Ramey, MA, Soc. Admn., is Associate Professor Emeritus, School of Social Work, The University of Akron, and General Secretary, Association for the Advancement of Social Work with Groups, Inc.

John S. Wodarski, PhD, is Director, Doctoral Program, and Janet S. Wattles Research Professor, School of Social Work, University of Buffalo, State University of New York.

Aaron R. Mann, PhD, is Associate Professor, School of Social Work, The University of Pittsburgh.

CONTRIBUTORS

Bing-Kong Choy, MSS, Lecturer, Department of Social Work and Social Administration, University of Hong Kong.

Larry E. Davis, PhD, Professor, The George Warren Brown School of Social Work, Washington University, St. Louis.

Doreen Elliott, PhD, Professor, School of Social Work, University of Texas at Arlington.

Juanita B. Hepler, PhD, Associate Professor, Department of Social Work, Boise State University, Boise, Idaho.

Hisashi Hirayama, DSW, Professor, College of Social Work, The University of Tennessee–Knoxville.

Kasumi K. Hirayama, DSW, Associate Professor, School of Social Work, The University of Connecticut.

Tom Hopkins, MA/CQSW, Consultant in Social Work Education and Group Work, Weymouth, Dorset, England.

MaryAnn Hosang, MSW, Clinical Director, Children of Substance Abuse Program, Hays/Caldwell Council on Alcohol and Drug Abuse, San Marcos, Texas.

Zoë Levitt, MSW, The Toronto Hospital, Toronto, Ontario.

Elizabeth Lewis, PhD, Professor Emeritus, Department of Social Work, Cleveland State University.

Elizabeth I. Lewis, MSW, The Toronto Hospital, Toronto, Ontario.

Nazneen S. Mayadas, DSW, Professor, School of Social Work, University of Texas at Arlington.

Joan K. Parry, PhD, Professor Emeritus of Social Work, College of Social Work, California State University-San Jose.

Kenneth E. Reid, PhD, Western Michigan University School of Social Work, Kalamazoo, Michigan.

John B. Turner, DSW, Wm. R. Kenan, Jr. Professor and Dean Emeritus, School of Social Work, The University of North Carolina at Chapel Hill.

Alvin Walter, DSW, Professor, Norfolk State University School of Social Work, Norfolk, Virginia.

Rowena Grice Wilson, DSW, Associate Professor, Norfolk State University School of Social Work, Norfolk, Virginia.

John S. Wodarski, PhD, Director, Doctoral Program, and Janet B. Wattles Research Professor, School of Social Work, University of Buffalo, State University of New York.

Bernard J. Wohl, MSW, Executive Director, Goddard-Riverside Community Center, New York City.

Board of Directors, 1990-1991

Andrew Malekoff, Associate Editor, North Shore Child and Family Guidance, Roslyn Heights, NY.

Symposia Chairpersons:

Linda Adler, 1990, School of Social Work, Barry University, Miami, FL.

John H. Ramey, 1991 (see General Secretary above).

Benj. L. Stempler, 1992, Atlanta, GA.

At-Large Members:

Margot Breton, Faculty of Social Work, University of Toronto, Toronto, Ontario.

Max Casper, School of Social Work, Syracuse University, Syracuse, NY.

Anita Curry-Jackson, Department of Social Work, Wright State University, Dayton, OH.

Ivor J. Echols, School of Social Work, University of Connecticut, West Hartford, CT.

Maeda J. Galinsky, School of Social Work, University of North Carolina, Chapel Hill, NC.

Alex Gitterman, School of Social Work, Columbia University, New York, NY.

Lillian C. Kimura, YWCA of the U.S.A., National Board, New York, NY.

Norma C. Lang, Faculty of Social Work, University of Toronto, Toronto, Ontario.

Elizabeth Lewis, Department of Social Work, Cleveland State University, Cleveland, OH.

1991 Symposium Planning Committee

John H. Ramey, School of Social Work, University of Akron, Akron, OH; Chair.

Arthur S. Biagianti, Librarian, Mandel School of Applied Social Sciences, Case Western Reserve University, Cleveland, OH; Chair, Book Exhibit.

Roslyn Birger-Hershfield, Akron, OH; Chair, Panel on Group Work in Diverse Settings – Non-US.

Raymond R. Brown, School of Social Work, University of Akron, Akron, OH; Chair, Honors, and Awards.

Marvin D. Feit, Director, School of Social Work, University of Akron, Akron, OH; Chair, Abstracts and Proceedings.

Fred F. Fuerst, YMCA of Metropolitan Akron, Akron, OH; Chair, Committee for Traditional Group Serving Agencies.

Deborah L. Hershfield, Akron, OH; Chair, Publicity Committee; Chair, Panel on Group Work in Diverse Settings in the USA.

James King, School of Social Work, University of Akron, Akron, OH; Chair, Institutes.

Douglas Kohl, Executive Director, YMCA of Metropolitan Akron, Akron, OH.

Elizabeth Lewis, School of Social Work, Cleveland State University, Cleveland, OH; Chair, Syllabus Exchange.

Aaron R. Mann, School of Social Work, University of Pittsburgh, Pittsburgh, PA.

John Mumper, Community Services Technology, University of Akron, Akron, OH; Chair, Arrangements and Volunteers.

Vernon L. Odom, Executive Director, Akron Community Service Center and Urban League, Akron, OH.

Ruby B. Pernell, Professor Emeritus, Mandel School of Applied Social Sciences, Case Western Reserve University, Cleveland, OH; Chair, Hospitality and Entertainment.

Jane Roberts, Coordinator, Social Services Technology, Wayne College, University of Akron, Orrville, OH.

Cazzell M. Smith, Sr., Executive Director, East Akron Community House; Member, Summit County Council, Akron, OH; Treasurer; Chair, Finance Committee.

Hyman L. Tabachnick, North Wayne, NJ; Chair, Registration Committee.

John S. Wodarski, Director, Doctoral Program, and Janet B. Wattles Research Professor, School of Social Work, University of Buffalo, State University of New York.

Introduction:
The Power of Diversity

Diversity is a fact in the middle of the 1990s and becoming increasingly important as we move into the twenty-first century. The questions and issues before us are how to deal with, adjust to, manage, or use constructively the power of diversity. The theme of the Thirteenth Annual Symposium on Social Work with Groups was to ask social workers to capture this power and be able to explore it from different aspects. The papers in this volume address this theme and illustrate the complexity, creativity, and excitement of the diversity concept.

The four keynote presentations stake out separate themes about diversity. The themes are then explored through articles pertaining to each one. The text concludes with a paper regarding group work content in the undergraduate and graduate curriculums of schools of social work.

Turner and Wodarski establish one of the main thrusts of the text by calling attention to viewing diversity from an environmental and macro system perspective. Each hits hard at the necessity for social group workers to be able to work effectively at the macro level. This theme is quite important and a departure from the usual thrust which is to illustrate group work in a clinical context. These authors demonstrate the value and importance of using social group work practice at the macro level.

Turner outlines the changing aspects of ethnic diversity and describes the inequality which minorities experience daily. Throughout his paper he presents experiences which illustrate the constant problems with not dealing with ethnic diversity and at the end suggests several action strategies to deal with this particular problem.

Wodarski looks at the economic and political context in which social group work takes place at the macro level. In his view social group work has not adequately addressed the macro perspective and as such its workers could have been more effective with clients. He wonders whether social group workers have the necessary knowledge, skills, and ability to act in the economic and political areas. He presents empirical data to support his contention and particularly notes that often individual change does not sustain past five years. He concludes that one of the more viable aspects of dealing with ethnic diversity is for social group work to concentrate on the economic and political context for improving our society.

Joan Parry and Larry Davis focus on the educational and practice dimensions of diversity. While Parry addresses educational issues in social work curriculum it is Davis who forthrightly confronts race and class as major practice issues.

Parry wonders where group work is in the generalists curriculum. In the past several years she has witnessed the diminution of social group work content in curriculums of schools of social work as they have concentrated on the generalist model of social work practice. She sees social group work as a major bridge in the relationship between macro and micro practice.

Davis talks directly about the crisis of diversity in our society. He explores why race and class will continue to have profound social and political implications for many years. For example, he notes that in the ensuing years the number of minorities will continue to increase yet our society remains largely segregated. Second, large segments of our society have become increasingly impoverished. At minimum, these two points illustrate the difficulty social workers will continue to face unless we deal directly with the crisis of diversity in our society. He sees social group work as a vital force because it plays a prominent role in both clinical and macro practice.

These three themes are then illustrated in the remaining articles in the text: (1) the changing aspects of our environment and the necessity to deal with inequality, (2) the macro system and its economic and political consequences, and (3) the teaching and practice issues emerging from the effects of race and class on practice.

In the relationship of the macro system and its effect on our practice there are three noteworthy articles. Choy illustrates how group work practice in Hong Kong has been largely influenced by the external environment, which consists mainly of the economic and social factors. His paper revives the dormant idea of social action and social change in social group work practice. Hepler describes how by improving the environment of children with learning disabilities you can also increase their social skills. She concentrates on developing a social skills program for the kids as well as trying to create a better environment for the children. Wohl's paper is a thorny issue. He wonders whether it is possible to relate what happens daily in a community center with the broader social societal issues, such as equity and justice. This issue forces us to confront whether we can relate social work practice to many controversial and larger social issues in our society, such as diversity.

A second theme examines client's impact upon their environment. In this context Hopkins illustrates how reminiscence group work is very effective. He sees this type of group work as being where one recalls past events and experiences in a supportive and sympathetic environment, which, in turn, leads to increased self-confidence and self-esteem of clients. This type of group work stresses the assets of older people by emphasizing individuality and identity. Hopkins, therefore, is working directly with the clients and feels that by increasing their self-confidence and self-esteem they can contribute more to their immediate environment and play a more significant role than they have as they continue to get older.

The third theme centers on the teaching of social group work, and addresses several different issues. For example, Wilson and Walter show how research can generate knowledge and be used to promote social group work practice. In their view social workers do not find research knowledge useful in solving practice problems. They illustrate how we can overcome this problem while teaching social group work. Hirayama and Hirayama address directly the use of self in implementing the concepts of power and empowerment. They believe that the concept of empowerment has been forgotten and they are trying to revive it. They illustrate how the social worker can use himself or herself in bringing to fruition the concept of power and empowerment in group work.

Reid's paper differentiates group work from case work. He is concerned about the notion of action in group work and feels that a combination of self-knowledge and action in group work empowers members to act upon their world. He concentrates on how the social group worker enables clients to develop this notion of self-knowledge and a healthy concept of action in order to effectively help clients deal with their external environment.

Mayadas and Elliott offer a unified theory of group work practice, based on a combination of general systems of social development perspectives. They feel that this unified theory will enable group work to retain its therapeutic position, while also reinstating the social into its repertoire and regain its lost heritage. They, too, recall some of social group works' past successes, and are concerned with how group work can be effective in today's curriculum climate.

The chapter by Lewis at the end of the text illustrates what is being taught in social work schools. She did a content analysis of 50 course outlines from 14 BSW programs and ten graduate programs in the U.S., Canada, Britain, Hong Kong, and Israel. In her review she finds an improved literature base since 1984, and confirms the observations made by the authors in this text. There needs to be a greater focus on social group work in the curriculums of schools of social work, as it has shifted in the past 15 to 20 years. This change has resulted in social group work almost becoming extinct. The papers in this text illustrate ways in which social group work can become more effective in the education of social work students and helping prepare professionals to deal more effectively with cultural diversity. Indeed, the emphasis and the message throughout this text and through each of the papers is that to deal effectively with today's problems and with the increasing impact of cultural diversity as we enter the twenty-first century social group work practice will need to be revived and emphasized.

Diversity appears to be a reality for which answers are constantly evolving. Research to inform practice is narrow or limited if it is not used, underutilized, misapplied or in the example of social work knowledge does lead to action. One of the more interesting problems presented in this text is whether we continue to emphasize work with clients and groups in helping them cope with their problems or do we use our knowledge and skills to help shape the environment in which many controversial phenomena, such as diversity, continue to be a potent force. The authors in this text clearly have a vision for social group workers to impact our environment as we also work with the client or the small group. Clearly then one issue before us is to place more emphasis on the macro system perspective of social group work practice, as we struggle to bring back to our curriculum content in social group work practice. A second issue, quite relevant to this text, is whether we can use our group work skills to capture the power of diversity and help shape the environment with our clients.

Chapter 1

Group Work and Ethnic Diversity

John B. Turner

The theme of this conference "capturing the power of diversity," though attractive, is more strongly resisted than supported by the general population. It is resisted because of the axiom that without sufficient inducements, what people with power want to do least is to share their power.

The issue is only partially defined by the phrase "capturing the power of diversity"; the other side of the issue is exploitation of the diversity by the powerful. To capture the power of diversity requires preventing and eliminating exploitation of those who are different.

This paper will outline changing aspects of ethnic diversity in America, describe inequality which minorities experience, and suggest action strategies for social group work.

PROFILE OF ETHNICS OF COLOR

Demographers are predicting an "explosion of ethnic population" in the USA by the year 2000. The phrase "EXPLOSION OF ETHNIC POPULATION" is only a slight overstatement calling attention to dramatic shifts in ethnic population now and in the future.

The bottom line is that people of color are increasing significantly in number; not just blacks, but also people of Hispanic origin,

Asian and Pacific Islanders, American Indians, including Eskimos and Aleutians, and other nonwhite races:

1. The white population as a percentage of the total U. S. population is decreasing. It dropped 3 percentage points between 1980 and 1990 and 8.3 percentage points between 1960 and 1990.
2. During the past decade, the black population was projected to grow by almost 3.5 million or to 12.1% of the total U.S. population. By the year 2010, the black population is projected to increase by nearly 10 million in comparison to its size in 1980.
3. The Hispanic population, between 1980 and 1990, grew by 7.3 million to 9.0 percent of the total U.S. population. By the year 2010 the Hispanic population is projected to increase by over 16 million in comparison with its size in 1980.
4. Between 1980 and 1990 the Asian population more than doubled, reflecting a growth in excess of 3.5 million.

The growth in the past decade for any one of these groups is larger than the population of most American cities. As one might expect, the growth has been uneven within as well as among states:

1. While the white population in actual numbers increased slightly in all but 14 states, the percentage of ethnic population increased in all but six states.
2. More than 41% of the population is nonwhite in California, Louisiana, South Carolina, Mississippi, and the District of Columbia. Demographers predict that California will be the first state with 50% of its population made up from ethnic backgrounds.
3. Approximately 25% of the population is nonwhite in New York, Texas, North Carolina, Georgia, Maryland, New Mexico, and Alaska.

By the year 2000, it is predicted that one out of every four Americans will be Asian, black, Hispanic, or Mid-Eastern. By 2010 it is highly possible that minorities of color will constitute the majority in 53 of America's 100 largest cities, with whites becoming the new minority with respect to size, but not with respect to influence.

Currently, Hispanics (after blacks) are by far the largest minority. It is projected that by 2015 Hispanics will grow in size to about 40 million people and will surpass the black population in size by the year 2020. Included under the umbrella term "Hispanic" are many subcultural groups: Mexicans (12 million); Puerto Ricans (3.3 million); Cubans (1 million); plus smaller numbers from Central and South American countries–Dominicans, El Salvadorians, Colombians, and people from Spain and Portugal. Hispanics are not, therefore, one cultural group, but several. The same can be said of Asians.

Two factors account for this phenomenal growth. First, the far greater source of ethnic population growth comes as a result of immigration, including persons who are admitted legally as well as those persons who enter illegally. Second, birth rates among minority populations are far higher than in the white majority.

In contrast with the 1960s when a majority of new Americans came from Europe, in 1985 only 11% of immigrants were from Europe, 46 percent were from Asian countries. Forty percent came from Latin American countries.

What we see then, as indicated earlier, is a significant increase in all minorities of color, especially in the larger cities and in selected states. We also see the numerical domination by blacks among minorities of color giving way to minorities of Hispanic origin.

A BRIEF NOTE ON PROBLEMS OF MINORITIES

Some minority leaders have felt that minority population growth would result in improved conditions for people of color, presumably by increasing the potential of minorities to advance their cause through use of the ballot. To date, the evidence does not support this line of reasoning.

If one looks at how well minorities of color are doing, there is good news and bad news. Minorities of color who qualify for middle-class status appear to keep up, although they continue to lag behind their white counterparts. Other minority persons tend to do significantly less well than their white counterparts. Ethnic and racial minorities are chronically over-represented in categories that reflect significantly lower life chances:

- Teenage pregnancies
- Low birth weight
- Poor health
- Poor education
- Drug and alcohol abuse
- Perpetrators and victims of violence
- The ill-housed
- The unemployed, underemployed, and the unemployable
- The poor
- Victims of psychosocial assaults

Consider children and poverty. First a few measurement points:

In 1989

- The poverty level for a family of four was $12,675;
- The poverty level for a single adult was $6,024;
- In 1989, the average poor family had a monthly income of $588, $400 below the poverty threshold.

Now

- Of the 15 million poor children in 1989* 7,599,000 or 50.8 percent were white; 14.8% of all white children were poor;
- 4,375,000 or 29.3% were black; 43.7% of all black children;
- 2,603,000 or 17.4% were Latino; 36.2% of all Latino children;
- 368,000 or 3.5% were Asian.

Between 1979 and 1989, the percentage in the number of poor children for each group was as follows:

- White children   22.7%
- Black children   14.1%
- Latino children   69.6%
- Asian children   23.0%

---

*CDF, *Child Poverty in America*. Youth and Family Futures Clearinghouse, 1991, p. 7.

Presently, white and Latino poverty rates among children are increasing faster than for blacks, Latino rates growing the fastest of the three. Within Latinos, Puerto Ricans are the hardest hit with poverty. Nearly half of all children joining the ranks of the poor between 1979 and 1989 were Latino.

Economic status is a good barometer of one's life chances. The data seem to suggest a worsening of economic status for many minority people between 1979 and 1989, and while the numbers of children in poverty increased for all groups, it increased substantially for minority groups.

If economic status can be used as a predictor of what can be concluded about other life chance areas, with a large increase in ethnic population, the impact will be to exacerbate the gap in life chances for a large number of minority people.

The quality of intergroup relations is another index of the well-being of racial and ethnic minorities. There are a number of signs that all is not well in this area. The nation, including universities and colleges is experiencing an increase in overt hostility.

For example, during the 1990 U. S. Senate race in North Carolina, the outcome of one race is thought to have been significantly influenced at the last minute, with the charge by the incumbent, that against his black opponent's support of affirmative action meant that minorities would be given preference in hiring for jobs. This charge promoted intergroup hostilities and is alleged to have swung a number of young white voters to support the incumbent.

In Germany, a key plank in the organization of 10,000 neo-Nazis called for sending immigrants of color back to their native homes. This issue has since been championed by mainline political candidates and leaders in Germany and in other European countries.

The lesson to be derived from the increase in open intergroup hostility is clear. While the fear and hostility have roots in multiple sources, a key factor which fuels these behaviors is competition for jobs. As long as intergroup relations rests upon an attitude held by the majority "that next to me I'm for you," and as long as the need for jobs with decent wages, is substantially more than the supply available and accessible, we can expect the stage to be set for overtly hostile intergroup relations.

How can the power of diversity be captured, how can we have a fair and just nation when our nation seems bent on investing in social and economic behaviors that keep the nation divided into two unequal Americas:

- One America that is white, and a second America made up of people of color, where there is diversity but little power.
- A white America that is for the most part comfortable and affluent; and a people of color America that is significantly less well off, including many people barely able to make ends meet.
- A white America with preferential access to jobs, to business opportunities, to better and more affordable housing and health care; and a second America of people of color restricted to low-paying employment with substantially less access to health care, to quality housing, and forced into a greater dependency upon welfare.
- A white America that sits at policy-making tables with full privileges, and a people of color America at policymaking tables as token members, if present at all.

After 200 years of democracy, we face the final decade of the century, with this visible and dramatic division in our society reflected in nearly every aspect of contemporary American life. The doctrine of separate and unequal as a function of racial and ethnic discrimination is still the dominating philosophy of social status in America. Although it is no longer the official law of the land, and despite gains by a few, whether held in place by tradition, ignorance, greed, and prejudice, it is the guiding private and public policy for determining the social and economic status of minorities of color.

Although a few business and political leaders understand that two Americas are expensive and injurious to the values, progress, and economic productivity of the nation, and, how this in turn influences the ability of the United States to be a top world leader, this unequal and immoral division continues to prevail.

Dividing our nation contributes to social problems and makes solutions more difficult in economic productivity, education, crime, health, housing, and governance. It results in an unhealthy inconsistency between our public and private behavior and the values espoused by our leaders and basic documents of the nation. The majority of our leaders, however, at all levels of community appear willing for the American people to pay the financial and social costs involved in maintaining two Americas.

Too often policy decisions are a consequence of a "we" and "them" approach. Social and economic policy decisions reflect an ongoing pattern of power exploitation by the "we" which effectively denies the "them"–the diverse opportunities to successfully invest in their own future. Equally disquieting is the accumulative impact of institutional racism upon ethnics of color. It destroys self-esteem, the drive toward self-help, motivation and generally weakens instrumental behavior to improve the quality of their lives.

It is not surprising, then, that minorities of color often look upon public policy as a deck stacked against them. From their perspective, community development and growth are viewed as being more against, than, for equal life chances and the provision table opportunities.

The twenty-first century is being ushered in by significant growth and diversity in and among ethnic minorities and by changes in the world of work which hold a potential for exacerbating social and economic deficits. These changes are likely to be accompanied by a greater degree of destructive competition and conflict within and among ethnic groups, and between ethnic and majority populations.

This situation, a continuing separation of the nation into two unequal Americas, changes in the requirements of the work force, and growth in the number and diversity of minorities pose significantly greater threats to minorities than in the past.

In 1948, Gunnar Myrdal wrote a significant book about and blacks and whites. It was called *The American Dilemma.* Today we have a new America Dilemma. It deals not just with blacks and whites, but all people of color and white Americans. It presents a challenge to all human service professions, but in particular to social work and to social group work as a method and as a field of practice.

There are a few signs that in the near future the winds of social change might help to create a more favorable climate within which to mitigate this situation. Definers of political ideology on the left and on the right are once again paying attention to domestic issues. If the advice of both ends of the ideological gauntlet is to make a difference with poor people, albeit through different approaches, it may signal the opening of a political debate that will permit consideration of policies of a social investment and social development nature in lieu of the continuing debate about legislating more or less welfare.

If the advice of such ideology is heeded, it may signal the opening of a political debate that will permit consideration of policies of a social investment and social development nature in lieu of the continuing debate about legislating more or less welfare.

Perhaps this increased sensitivity will reinforce the publicly declared mandate of a democratic society for government and private sectors to more adequately design and provide programs and policies that support investment in the good life by all of its citizens, thus, more equitable life chances for all.

Another source of support for a change in the climate to extend equality in life chances to people of color may come from changes that are thought to be taking place in the behavior of some of the middle class. Some futurists are predicting the 1990s will usher in a definite move–of the young and more privileged–away from the "me" decade of the 1980s toward the "decency" decade in the 1990s.

Social trend spotters predict that, "As the need for display of status diminishes, Americans will be looking for visible virtue." There will be "more of a concern with giving to society." To the extent that these prognostications are correct, they should produce a climate sympathetic to a consideration of more effective initiatives for helping to promote social justice and social development, and to programs aimed at the prevention of human waste.

The nation may be approaching a point in its history when the "left" and the "right" are coming closer together in understanding the causes and threats of social discontent and instability and the costs of racism to the social and economic future of all citizens.

At the core of the policy strategy must be the objective of preventing poverty and aiding people to escape poverty. A second objective involves insistence on humane responsiveness and competence from public institutions in addressing the affairs of people of color especially in areas of health care, criminal justice, and public education.

To achieve these policy objectives will require making them a part of political campaigns on local, state, and national levels; it will require relentless pursuit of legal redress in support of individual rights; it will require linking the benefits of social policy to corporate self-interests and recruitment of corporate leaders, and, it will require public recognition and support for those who work in behalf of these objectives.

Because policy strategy requires coalitions at all levels, social group work has a special role it can play due to its day-to-day proximity and contact with the disadvantaged, especially people of color. One role should be that of social informants constantly making the public aware of the impact and costs of poverty, poor housing, poor health, and poor service. Also, it should help the public to know "what works" and what doesn't work in redressing these problems.

A second major strategy for closing the gap in life chances calls for providing developmental assistance to children and youth. It is a strategy in which group work agencies historically have played a unique and essential role. In 1949, Ryland and Wilson wrote that "most social agencies serving groups have two purposes in common: (1) to help individuals use groups to further their development into emotionally balanced, intellectually free, and physically fit persons; and (2) to help groups achieve ends desirable in an economic, political and social democracy."

This is the kind of help all children and their families need. Such service is especially valuable to the disadvantaged child and family of color. Programs should aim to help children to successfully navigate the transitions from home to school; from school to work; from home to citizenship; from life as a single person to being responsible for a family, to full and productive membership in society.

What is needed is a return of the Henry Streets, the Chicago Commons, Emerson Houses, the Alta and Goodrich Houses, the Friendly Inns. What is needed is a return of settlement houses. Settlements provided ownership of a place, a safe haven, a collective locality based and subculture home. It provided mediation, education, protection, intergenerational dialogue, connections between present reality and future aspirations. It provided practical solutions to practical problems as a basis for more substantial personal help. The settlement was available 24 hours, during and after school and on weekends.

What settlements did was to work with families and peer cultures, to see that youth and young adults, had:

1. Marketable skills; and capacity to think and reason;
2. Healthy bodies and minds;
3. Competency and comfort in communicating with others;
4. Understanding of how one's family, community, city, and state operate;
5. Successful experience in working to bring about change and betterment in one's life and in causes outside of, or bigger than, one's self;
6. Appreciation of art, music, and the theater;
7. Understanding of history, man and the universe, including an appreciation of one's cultural history;
8. An appreciation for the ability to contribute to one's family and to experience the love and care of a family;
9. Success in school and in the world of work, and
10. A grounding in ethics.

A more supportive, less corrosive social, economic, and physical environment and youth with strong reality-based self-esteem are the two requirements for a more successful struggle against ethnic and racial discrimination.

To play this role, group work agencies must:

1. Convince the public and funding agencies that there are no quick fixes;
2. Use methods to deal with practical needs of children and families as well;
3. Emphasize greater concern with the social development of children and families and the prevention of handicapping conditions;
4. Develop, maintain, and strengthen linkages of their clientele with external sources of influence.

A business-as-usual approach to ethnic diversity and significant growth in minority populations pose troublesome quality-of-life issues in the future of many people of color, and they pose major challenges to policy makers, to applied social scientists, and to human service professionals such as teachers and social workers.

If significant progress is to be made toward elimination of the gap-in-life changes, social policy and the provision of developmental assistance must relentlessly pursue objectives which help to make the social and economic environment no more hostile or alien to people of color than it is to other Americans. The nation must endeavor to create a level playing field for the formulation of public policy. Toward this end it is not in the best interest of the country for the status of people of color to remain hostage to the debate of liberal versus conservative politics.

It will take many groups and professions working solo and in concert to accomplish significant progress in closing the gap-in-life chances, but social group work can play a pivotable role.

Chapter 2

Social Group Work, Social Action in the Twenty-First Century Economic and Political Context

John S. Wodarski

SUMMARY. Issues in contemporary social group work are reviewed. The discussion centers on the context of current social group work, group level variables, components of effective group reward structures, issues for the theoretical development of social group work, competency criteria, macrolevel analysis, prevention, and implementation of intervention strategy. Where relevant, examples are provided.

In response to an increasing demand for accountability in the delivery of social services, social work educators, researchers, and practitioners have called for the establishment of social work services on a more empirical basis. Likewise, there is an apparent need for the more objective evaluation of services in order to assess whether client needs are being adequately met. The demand for definite criteria of change, delineation of change methods, evaluation of the effects of the change methods, and education planned on a more rational basis should ultimately improve the quality of social service provided (Wodarski, Thyer, Iodice, & Pinkston, 1991). Despite the substantial amount of research examining the effectiveness of traditional social work practice methods, there have been relatively few investigations to assess the effectiveness of traditional instructional methodologies employed in the preparation of social work practitioners (Constable, 1978; Sowers-Hoag & Thyer, 1985; Wodarski, 1979, 1986). In 1973 Briar called for the use of 20% of all social services budgets to conduct research on the effectiveness of social work practice. A similar commitment among schools of social work to the evaluation of instruction seems also advisable. If data which calls into question the effectiveness of traditional practice continue to accumulate, the process of educating practitioners must eventually be examined to alleviate possible deficiencies in training (Wodarski, 1986). The rationale for the evaluation of the educational process is based upon two major factors: first being the conflictual data base concerning the effectiveness of social services, and second, the NASW Code of Ethics which specifies that practitioners should employ interventions based on the most efficacious, data-based theories (NASW, 1980). Better conceptualizations are required of the group skills social work education should provide its students (Paulus, 1989). Further research is necessary to determine how to most effectively teach generalized practice skills and specific advanced interpersonal change technologies.

Social work education today reflects a sixty-year effort to move away from outdated definitions of practice as these prove inadequate to meet societal needs, and to reconceptualize the profession on a continual basis. Many curriculum models, like practice models, exist but few have been adequately tested (Wodarski, Thyer, Iodice, & Pinkston, 1991).

Group therapy has been shown to have therapeutic power, and in certain situations it may even have uniquely curative value. However, many members of the helping professions have had little or no exposure to group work either in their academic or in their professional careers. Although social workers are in the large majority among all clinicians, Middleman (1978) said it is a myth that schools of social work are offering students equal opportunities to learn both individual and group methods of helping. If so, practicing therapists with little familiarity with groups may wonder what such groups are all about, and this essay will attempt to answer certain of the questions that naturally occur–the who, what, when, and why of group treatment.

Volumes have been written about the variables to be touched upon here, but, regrettably, other questions remain largely unanswerable. This effort will be a beginning, and for the rest, Hartford (1978) summed up the case by quoting an unnamed colleague: "The only way you can learn about groups is experientially" (p. 8), which reads like an open invitation for us to get involved in group work and to see for ourselves.

CONTEXT: ECONOMIC AND POLITICAL

Social workers are operating in new complex environments in terms of knowledge and technological explosions. Within the last two decades, the United States industrial economy has changed to an economy based on information technology. Social workers must be equipped to deal with the issues that force chage on our society, i.e., being competitive in world markets, responding to new markets, management of environmental concerns, increasing industrial productivity, technological transfer activities, and so forth. In addition, exploding technologies, in both the hard sciences and computer fields, contribute significantly to the environment in which the country finds itself (Latour, 1987; Callon, Law, & Rip, 1986). Most new employment research centers on the complex issues that face society, such as the development of new sources of energy, new industrial technologies, health care and the elderly, and development of adequate food supplies. This emphasis comes about because the body of knowledge in each of these areas is constantly changing and growing.

In the manufacturing economy of the twentieth century, the nation's industries have concentrated on production. For many years, this approach has been eminently successful in building a powerful economy and a high quality of life. But there is strong evidence that the world economy has shifted away from a materials and labor intensive foundation toward one relying on technology for real growth.

Whatever the source of the past's failures, the attitude of industry is now quite different. Corporations of all sizes are hungry for new technology and are becoming more adept every day in integrating it into new products and processes. Industry is now seeking to recognize new approaches earlier in the stream of knowledge (Carnevale, 1991; Eisenberger, 1989). Social workers must use their skills to help clients develop behaviors that make them employable.

GROUP LEVEL VARIABLES

Within the last decade research results have indicated that group cohesion, commitment, performance, and effectiveness are related to the reward structure of the groups. Recently, there have begun to appear in the education and psychology literatures a series of related small-group team techniques based on behavioral analysis that appear to have great promise in changing the basic structure of the group to achieve positive effects on many group dimensions at the same time, such as performance, leadership effectiveness, cohesion, acceptance and liking of group members, norms, conformity proneness, power, acquisition of relevant skills, and commitment to group goals. These small-group techniques are known by various names, but they are referred to here as group reward structures, because they all involve individuals working in cooperative teams on group performance tasks (Boocock, 1978; Buckholdt & Wodarski, 1978). These techniques are unique in that they apply social psychological principles of reward interdependence developed in laboratory work and short-term experimentation to the development of practical group procedures. Group reward structures set up a situation in which the relevant group behavior of each individual furthers group goals. This in turn has been shown to increase individual support for group performance, to increase group performance itself under a variety of circumstances, and to increase the frequency of relevant social behaviors, particularly interracial and gender liking.

COMPONENTS OF EFFECTIVE GROUP
REWARD STRUCTURES

Given, then, that the reward structure of the group is at least one of the most important manipulable features of group process that can facilitate effective problem solving, how should an ideal system be constructed? Literature in educational and organizational psychology indicates that certain reward structures can facilitate group cohesion, leader effectiveness, productivity, and group effectiveness. In applying the principles it is given that tasks have been chosen that are appropriate to the ability level of the group members, and are attractive and feasible. The social worker should analyze the following points in developing a relevant reward system:

1. Appropriate behavior must be reinforced. The failure of pass-fail experiments in universities (Johnson, 1975; Travers, 1977) should lay to rest the notion that students study for the sake of learning alone; they also study because they are rewarded for studying and if they are not rewarded for study the incidence of this behavior will be quite low (Bandura, 1969). Thus appropriate social behavior in groups will occur only when members gain sufficient reinforcement (rewards) from peers and the leader. Disruptive behavior, a major problem in groups, will decrease when it is not reinforced and leaders therefore must structure rewards that are contingent upon appropriate behavior. Token economies are one example of ways in which appropriate behaviors that are to be reinforced can be made highly specific (Kazdin, 1978; Wodarski & Bagarozzi, 1979).

2. Reinforcers must be available to all members, but not too easily available. As obvious as this sounds, this is the major failing of traditional reward systems. For many members, the chances of reaching an acceptable goal are exactly nil. Other members can achieve these rewards without much effort. In these circumstances, it is hardly surprising that a substantial number of members turn themselves off as learners and do only what is required to be a member; which at most is not much (Schultz & Sherman, 1976). Thus, reinforcement systems must be structured in such a manner as to require effort according to each member's ability to attain the criterion.

3. Reinforcers (feedback) should be delivered close in time to the occurrence of the behavior they reinforce to be maximally effective. For younger members, less able members, and members who have not yet learned to delay gratification, a reward delivered every six or nine weeks is not feasible. Such members may decide that re-

wards are determined primarily by fate, by leader eccentricities, or the like. Even with a clear intellectual understanding of where rewards come from it is terribly hard for anyone to "turn over a new leaf" and maintain an improved level of performance for six, nine, or twelve weeks. Even when this is possible, the reward system may not be sensitive enough to recognize and reinforce an increase in performance level in a member who has been a low performer. Accumulated research indicates that feedback is one of the most significant variables increasing individual performace in a group (Andrasik, Heimberg, & McNamara, 1981). Feedback on group tasks initially should occur daily and should be faded (phased out) as members acquire necessary social and academic skills. Feedback can occur through credits on posters and charts, in daily newsletters, and so forth.

4. Recent studies indicate that members must know what behaviors are going to be reinforced and how often; i.e., structure facilitates the attainment of group goals. Additionally, leaders must be consistent in their application of reward systems. Data show conclusively that inconsistent application leads to ineffective acquisition of relevant academic and social behaviors and an increase in the probability of disruptive behaviors. Therefore, contingencies must be specified in such a manner that members understand what is involved in securing rewards (DeRisi & Butz, 1975). Members should possess a record, preferably in written form, of the reward system that is in operation. In many instances the communications can occur in contract form.

5. The type of reinforcer chosen may not be appropriate for the individual. That is, the reinforcer may be weak compared to other reinforcers that are currently maintaining the behavior. Three critical questions center on how appropriate the incentives are. How much of the reinforcer has the member had in the past? How much does the member currently possess? How much of the reinforcer do other members around him/her possess? The power of the reinforcer is inversely related to the answer to all three of these questions. For example, the reinforcer may be appropriate but the amount is not proportional to the effort involved in changing the behavior. Likewise, the amount or the size of the reinforcer may be appropriate but the reinforcer is not provided at a high enough frequency or

the schedule of reinforcement is too erratic to override the cost involved in the member's changing the behavior. Leaders can isolate relevant reinforcement by asking the members what they would like, observing them in free time periods, and giving them the Reinforcement Survey (Cautela, 1972; Cautela & Kastenbaum, 1967). Such research ensures that the leader possesses the requisite information for structuring an effective reinforcement system.

6. The appropriate reinforcers and delivery conditions are sufficient, but there has been no isolation of those significant others in the member's environment who are providing the reinforcement that maintains the behavior and who may in fact be punishing behaviors that are being reinforced. Also, the significant others chosen to participate in the modification plan may be inconsistently applying the agreed-upon plan of behavioral change or may not be attractive enough to facilitate the behavioral changes. Leaders should isolate existing peer group reinforcement patterns and structure reinforcement systems to encourage peer support for appropriate group behavior (Wodarski, 1980).

ISSUES FOR THE THEORETICAL DEVELOPMENT OF SOCIAL GROUP WORK

It is evident that more elaborate theories of human behavior are needed to provide the rationale for complex therapeutic intervention systems that are based on principles derived from empirical knowledge, with the goal being to help the client achieve behavior change and its maintenance. These theories must consider biological, sociological, economic, political, and psychological factors as they interact in the human matrix to cause behavior. It is a definite challenge for any theory of human behavior to isolate those components that are responsible for behavior change, such as the specific aspects of a treatment package in terms of expectations for change, role of cognitive processes, particular client and social worker characteristics, interventions, context of intervention, and so forth. Once this knowledge is developed, the choice of behavioral alteration techniques can be made on such criteria as client and therapist characteristics, context of therapeutic intervention, and type of intervention. For example, the complexity of the behavioral approach is evidenced in regard to the application of the rather elementary procedures based on the principles of positive reinforcement. In conjunction with the client, the social worker must decide what positive reinforcers will be used, who will administer them, where they will be employed and with what frequency and what additional techniques are needed to change the behavior.

Recent evidence suggests that, in order for behavioral change to be successful, macro-level intervention variables have to be considered. An adequate theory of human behavior will isolate the social system variables (i.e., legal, political, health, financial, social services, educational, housing, employment, etc.) and their effect on human behavior. Moreover, these variables have to be addressed in a manner that focuses on the attainment of generalization and maintenance of behavior. Current theories fall far short of this goal. This focus on the maintenance of behavioral change will characterize sophisticated and effective human behavior theories (Wodarski, 1980).

COMPETENCY CRITERIA

As the demand for group workers increases, the training of practitioners will have to be formalized and competency criteria will have to be developed. Few places in the country offer concrete training. We will have to streamline existing training programs since social group work is an extremely complex technology to apply and substantial time is needed to develop requisite skills for implementing the procedures in a comprehensive and competent manner. We must determine where to train practitioners and what level of skills must be acquired at each educational degree level. That is, what are the basic training functions at the undergraduate level, at the master's level, and the doctoral level? We will need to develop concrete entrance criteria for students who will become social group workers as well as appropriately defined objectives for training. Also, testing procedures will have to be developed and incorporated into training programs to ensure that students meet appropriate standards. Such an assessment process will ensure that the individuals who call themselves social group workers are in fact competent to practice the techniques (Arkava & Brennen, 1975; Armitage & Clark, 1975; Peterson, 1976).

MACROLEVEL ANALYSIS

It is likely that future research will begin to unravel the complex relationship between societal experiences and human behavior. How we can construct a society with macrolevel interventions as opposed to individual interventions to prevent or facilitate certain behavior has been virtually ignored by the field. For example, social policies with provision of incentives for welfare clients who can work to secure and maintain employment, designing physical environments in such a manner that the probability of criminal behavior is decreased, and so on, must be examined. One example of an environmental design to facilitate the occurrence of a particular behavior is the "open schools" concept. In the open classroom the purpose is to increase social interaction among children and adults. The crucial questions center on how to structure environments that will support behavioral change achieved through interpersonal approaches, that is, provide enough reinforcers to maintain prosocial behavior, and what behaviors can be altered directly through macrolevel intervention (Kelly, Snowden, & Munoz, 1977).

PREVENTION

Social group work will place more emphasis on prevention, a major issue to be considered as the helping professions have a history of dealing with individuals only after they have exhibited problematic behaviors rather than before problematic behavior occurs. Some may wonder if we can really alter clients' behaviors after 20, 40, or 60 years of learning. Our task, therefore, is to facilitate the preventive and educative roles that can be assumed by social workers. We should develop criteria for early intervention. Prototypes of such an approach may be found in courses on parental effectiveness, sex education, marital enrichment, and so on. Such courses should focus on helping parents develop better communica-

tion and consistent child management skills, two variables research
has shown are necessary conditions for successful child rearing
(Hoffman, 1977), and helping prepare young adults for the requi-
sites of marriage, with effective communication skills, problem-
solving strategies, and conflict resolution procedures (Wodarski &
Wodarski, in press).

SOCIAL NETWORKS

Data suggest that adolescents are at less social risk to develop
mental distress if they are socially connected to other peers, i.e.,
social supports buffer stress, support and help individuals through
crisis periods, promote good physical health, and facilitate the acquisition and maintenance of relevant social competencies (Heller
& Swindle, 1983; Thyer, 1987; Wahler & Graves, 1983).

One of the most perplexing yet critical problems confronting
social work professionals interested in prevention is the effective
use of networking for adolescents at risk. Questions that need to be
resolved include the following: How can adolescents be tied to the
networks available in their peer communities? What peer characteristics may be matched with adolescent attributes to facilitate networking and enhancement of the individual's functioning? What
support systems such as the church, extended family, and friends
are available to enhance the adolescent's networks?

This aspect of prevention would involve development of programs to utilize efficacious and cost-effective assessment procedures to isolate physical, psychological, and social factors that lead
to networking. Possible procedures include: (1) assessment of the
adolescent's attributes such as homogeneity of peers, social cohesion, and services available; (2) enlistment of social networks and
support groups such as family, peers, ministers, and significant
adult models to provide necessary support; (3) preparation of the
adolescent in terms of emphasizing appropriate social behaviors
that will be rewarded and will facilitate integration into the social
structure of their peer community; (4) educating the adolescent
about support services available and whom to contact and gradually
introducing the individual to appropriate available support systems;

(5) developing appropriate preventive intervention; and (6) how social group work can facilitate such processes.

IMPLEMENTATION OF INTERVENTION STRATEGY: WHERE, BY WHOM, WHY, HOW LONG, AND ON WHAT LEVEL?

Context of Behavioral Change

Unfortunately, if a client exhibits a problematic behavior in one social context, such as school, the change strategies all too frequently are provided in another social context, such as a child guidance clinic, family service agency, or community mental health center. Such procedures create many structural barriers to effective intervention (Kazdin, 1977; Stokes & Baer, 1977). Data indicates that, if possible, preventive intervention should be provided in the same context where problematic behaviors are exhibited. If prevention change strategies are implemented in other contexts, the probabilities are reduced that learned behaviors can be sufficiently generalized and maintained.

Considerable study is needed to delineate those variables that facilitate the generalization and maintenance of behavior change. These may include choosing behaviors that will be maintained by the community support networks, substituting "naturally occurring" reinforcers, training relatives or significant others in the client's environment, gradually removing or fading contingencies, varying the conditions of training using different schedules of reinforcement, using delayed reinforcement and self-control procedures, and so forth (Kazdin, 1975, 1977). Such considerations equip social group workers in developing sophisticated and effective social service delivery systems which increase the probability of clients securing the necessary services to maintain themselves within their communities (Wodarski, 1980).

By Whom Should Change Be Delivered?

We have evidence to suggest that personal characteristics of social workers involved in prevention facilitate the delivery of services to clients. The worker should have similar attributes to facilitate the acceptance and subsequent participation in services provided (Ewing, 1974; Kadushin, 1972; Korchin, 1980; Thompson & Cimbolic, 1978). Other givens which research supports are: workers should be reinforcing individuals with whom adolescents can identify; they should possess empathy, unconditional positive regard, interpersonal warmth, verbal congruence, confidence, acceptance, trust, verbal ability, and physical attractiveness; and they should take time with adolescents and provide them the rationale for the services (Wodarski, 1987). Likewise, Bandura (1977), Rosenthal (1966), and Rosenthal and Rosnow (1969) have suggested that the worker's expectation of positive change in clients is also necessary. Additional research suggests that a behavioral change agent should have considerable verbal ability, should be motivated to help others change, should possess a wide variety of social skills, and should have adequate social adjustment (Berkowitz & Graziano, 1972; Gruver, 1971).

If the group worker chooses to employ an adolescent's parents, teachers, peers, or others as change agents, he/she must realize that they will have to assess at the very least how motivated these individuals are to help alleviate the dysfunctional behavior and how consistently they will apply techniques, what means are available to monitor the implementation of intervention to ensure that it is appropriately applied, and if the chosen change agent possesses characteristics such as similar social attributes, similar sex, and so forth that could facilitate the client's identification with him/her (Wodarski, 1989).

Rationale for Service Provided

The rationale for offering a program should be based primarily on empirical grounds. The decision-making process should reflect that the workers have considered what type of agency should house the service, that they have made an assessment of the organizational characteristics of the treatment context, and that the interests of the agency personnel have been considered in planning the service. A number of additional questions should also be posited to ensure the provision of relevant services. How can the program be implemented with minimal disruption? What new communication structures need to be used? What types of measurements can be used in evaluating the service? What accountability mechanisms need to be set up? What procedures can be utilized for monitoring the execution of the program (Feldman & Wodarski, 1974, 1976; Wodarski, 1981; Wodarski & Feldman, 1974)?

Duration

Few empirical guidelines exist regarding how long a service should be provided, that is, when client behavior has improved sufficiently in terms of quality and quantity, to indicate that services are no longer necessary. While much is said about termination, in the social work literature no criteria exist that can guide the process of terminating an intervention. We need to establish appropriate criteria for determining what are appropriate levels of frequency and quality of behaviors to facilitate the decision-making process of termination. Such criteria should be established before the service is to be provided and these should indicate how the program will be evaluated. The criteria should enable workers to determine whether or not a service is meeting the needs of the client. Moreover, they should help reveal the particular factors involved in deciding whether or not a service should be terminated. The more complete the criteria, the less this process will be based on subjective factors. In answering such questions workers realize that theory, intervention, and evaluation are all part of one total interventive process in prevention.

Larger Units for Social Change to Effect Prevention

Even broadly defined social policy decisions can directly affect the behaviors that will be exhibited by clients. For example, certain economic policy decisions (e.g., those pertinent to teenage employment and education, housing, and other social phenomena) have a determinate effect on behaviors that clients will exhibit in the future. A decision to adopt a full employment policy will obviously affect clients. Likewise, a national children's rights policy would ensure that each child is provided with adequate housing, education, justice, mental and social services, and so forth. Thus, the target for change may well be an institution or policy rather than the clients themselves.

If following a community analysis, a worker decides that a client is exhibiting appropriate behaviors for his/her social context and he/she determines that a treatment organization or institution is not providing adequate support for appropriate behaviors, or that it is punishing appropriate behavior, the group worker must then decide to engage in organizational or institutional change (Prunty, Singer, & Thomas, 1977). This may involve changing a social policy or a current bureaucratic means of dealing with people, or employing other strategies. In order to alter an organization, workers will have to study its components and assess whether or not they have the power to change these structures so that the client can be helped. In social work practice the primary focus has been on changing the individual. Future conceptualization should provide various means of delineating how human behavior can be changed by interventions on multilevels (Wodarski, 1977). Thus, workers should learn that following such a framework of human behavior, an "inappropriate" behavior exhibited by a client must be examined according to who defined it as inappropriate and where requisite interventions should take place. The obvious question that will face the social worker is how to coordinate these multilevel interventions.

Interventions at the macro level are increasingly more critical in light of follow-up data collected five years later on antisocial children who participated in a year-long behavior modification program which produced extremely impressive behavioral changes in the children. Results indicate that virtually none of the positive changes were maintained (McCombs, Filipczak, Friedman, & Wodarski, 1978; McCombs, Filipczak, Rusilko, Koustenis, & Wodarski, 1977). Possibly, maintenance could be improved when change is also directed at macro levels which would provide the necessary support for changed behavior.

CONCLUSION

In the coming years we will witness more interventions with clients that take a social group work focus. This manuscript has focused on the following issues and how they relate to effective services for clients: context, economic and political, group level variables, components of effective group reward structures, issues for the theoretical development of social group work, competency criteria, macrolevel analysis, prevention, social networks, and implementation of intervention strategies. The cost to clients from a social perspective and to our society from an economic perspective is substantial. If we do not utilize preventive group work interventions, we as a society will pay a great price.

REFERENCES

Andrasik, F., Heimberg, J. S., & McNamara, J. R. Behavior modification of work and work-related problems. (1981) In M. Hersen, R. Eisler, & P. Miller (Eds.), *Progress in behavior modification* (Vol. 11). New York: Academic.

Arkava, M. L., & Brennen, E. C. (1975). Toward a competency examination for the baccalaureate social work. *Journal of Education for Social Work, 11*(3), 22-29.

Armitage, A., & Clark, F. W. (1975). Design issues in the performance based curriculum. *Journal of Education for Social Work, 11*(1), 22-29.

Bandura, A. (1969). *Principles of behavior modification.* New York: Holt, Rinehart & Winston.

Bandura, A. (1977). *Social learning theory.* Englewood Cliffs, New Jersey: Prentice-Hall.

Berkowitz, B. P., & Graziano, A. N. (1972). Training parents as behavior therapists: A review. *Behavior Research and Therapy, 10*, 297-317.

Boocock, S. S. The social organization of the classroom. (1978). In R. H. Turner, J. Coleman, & R. C. Fox (Eds.), *Annual review of sociology.* Palo Alto: Annual Reviews.

Briar, S. (1973). The age of accountability. *Social Work, 18*, 114.

Buckholdt, D., & Wodarski, J. S. (1978). The effects of different reinforcement systems on cooperative behavior exhibited by children in classroom contexts. *Journal of Research and Development in Education, 12*(1), 50-68.

Callon, M., Law, J. & Rip, A. (1986). *Mapping the dynamics of science and technolgy: Sociology of science in the real world.* New York: Macmillan.

Carnevale, A. P. (1991). *America and the new economy.* San Francisco: Jossey-Bass.

Cautela, J. R. (1972). Reinforcement survey schedule: Evaluation and current applications. *Psychological Reports,* 683-690.

Cautela, J. R., & Kastenbaum, R. (1967). A reinforcement survey schedule for use in therapy, training, and research. *Psychological Reports, 20*, 1115-1130.

Constable, R. T., (1978). New directions in social work education: The task force reports. *Journal of Education for Social Work, 14*(1), 23-30.

DeRisi, W., & Butz, G. (1975). *Writing behaviorial contracts.* Champaign, IL: Research Press.

Eisenberger, R. (1989). *Reversing the decline of the American work ethic.* New York: Paragon House.

Ewing, T. N. (1974). Racial similarity of client and counselor and client satisfaction with counseling. *Journal of Counseling Psychology, 21*(5), 446-449.

Feldman, R. A., & Wodarski, J. S. (1974). Bureaucratic constraints and methodological adaptations in community-based research. *American Journal of Community Psychology, 2,* 211-224.

Gruver, G. G. (1971). College students as therapeutic agents. *Psychological Bulletin, 76,* 111-127.

Hartford, M. E. (1978). Groups in the human services: Some facts and fancies. *Social Work with Groups, 1,* 7-13.

Heller, K., & Swindle, R. W. (1983). Social networks, perceived social support, and coping with stress. In R. Felner, L. Jason, J. Moritsugu, & S. Farber (Eds.), *Preventive psychology: Theory, research, and practice.* New York: Pergamon Press.

Hoffman, M. L. (1977). Personality and social development. In M. Rosenzweig & L. Porter (Eds.), *Annual review of psychology.* Palo Alto, CA: Annual Reviews.

Johnson, J. M. (Ed.). (1975). *Behavior modification and technology in higher education.* Springfield, IL: Charles C Thomas.

Kadushin, A. (1972). The racial factor in the interview. *Social Work, 17*(3), 88-98.

Kazdin, A. E. (1975). *Behavior Modification in Applied Settings.* Homewood, IL: Dorsey Press.

Kazdin, A. E. (1977). *The token economy.* New York: Plenum Press.

Kazdin, A. E. (1978). The application of operant techniques in treatment rehabilitation and education. In S. L. Garfield & A. E. Bergin (Eds.), *Handbook of psychotherapy and behavior change: An empirical analysis.* New York: Wiley.

Kelly, J. G., Snowden, L. R., & Munoz, R. F. (1977). Social and community intervention. In M. R. Rosenzweig, & L. W. Porter (Eds.), *Annual review of psychology.* Palo Alto, CA: Annual Review.

Korchin, S. J. (1980). Clinical psychology and minority problems. *American Psychologist, 35*(3), 262-269.

Latour, B. (1987). *Science in action: How to follow scientists and engineers through society.* Cambridge, Massachusetts: Harvard University Press.

McCombs, D., Filipczak, J., Friedman, R. M., & Wodarski, J. S. (1978). Long-term follow-up of behavior modification with high risk adolescents. *Criminal Justice and Behavior, 5,* 21-34.

McCombs, D., Filipczak, J., Rusilko, S., Koustenis, G., & Wodarski, J. S. (1977, December). *Follow-up on behavioral development with disruptive juveniles in public schools.* Paper presented at the 11th Annual Meeting of the Association for the Advancement of Behavior Therapy, Atlanta, Georgia.

Middleman, R. R. (1978). Returning group processes to group work. *Social Work with Groups, 1,* 15-26.

National Association of Social Workers. (1980). *Code of ethics.* Silver Spring, Maryland: NASW.

Paulus, P. B. (1989). *Psychology of group influence (2nd ed.)* Hillsdale, New Jersey: Erlbaum.

Peterson, G. W. (1976). A strategy for instituting competency based education in large colleges and universities: A pilot program. *Educational Technology, 16*(12), 30-34.

Prunty, H. E., Singer, T. L., & Thomas, L. A. (1977). Confronting racism in inner-city schools. *Social Work, 22*(3), 190-194.

Rosenthal, R. (1966). *Experimenter effects in behavioral research.* New York: Appleton-Century-Crofts.

Rosenthal, R., & Rosnow, R. L. (Eds.). (1969). *Artifact in behavioral research.* New York: Academic.

Schultz, C. B., & Sherman, R. H. (1976). Social class, development and differences in reinforcer effectiveness. *Review of Educational Research, 46*, 25-59.

Sowers-Hoag, K. M., & Thyer, B. A. (1985). Teaching social work practice: A review and analysis of empirical research. *Journal of Social Work Education, 21*(3), 5-15.

Stokes, T. F., & Baer, D. M. (1977). An implicit technology of generalization. *Journal of Applied Behavior Analysis, 12*, 349-367.

Thompson, R. A., & Cimbolic, P. (1978). Black students' counselor preference and attitudes toward counseling center use. *Journal of Counseling Psychology, 25*(6), 570-575.

Thyer, B. A. (1987). Community-based self-help groups for the treatment of agoraphobia. *Journal of Sociology and Social Welfare, 14*(3), 135-141.

Travers, R. (Ed.) (1977). *Second handbook of research and teaching.* Chicago, IL: Rand McNally.

Wahler, R. G., & Graves, M. G. (1983). Setting events in social networks: Ally or enemy in child behavior therapy? *Behavior Therapy, 14*(1), 19-36.

Wodarski, J. S. (1977). The application of behavior modification technology to the alleviation of selected social problems. *Journal of Sociology and Social Welfare, 4*(7), 1055-1073.

Wodarski, J. S. (1979). Critical issues in social work education. *Journal of Education for Social Work, 15*(2), 5-13.

Wodarski, J. S. (1980). Procedures for the maintenance and generalization of achieved behavioral change. *Journal of Sociology and Social-Welfare, 7*(2), 298-311.

Wodarski, J. S. (1981). *The role of research in clinical practice.* Baltimore: University Park Press.

Wodarski, J. S. (1987). *Social work practice with children and adolescents.* Springfield, Illinois: Charles C Thomas.

Wodarski, J. S. (1986). *An introduction to social work education.* Springfield, Illinois: Charles C Thomas.

Wodarski, J. S. (1989). *Preventive health services for adolescents.* Springfield, Illinois: Charles C Thomas.

Wodarski, J. S., & Bagarozzi, D. (1979). *Behavioral social work.* New York: Human Sciences Press.

Wodarski, J. S., & Feldman, R. A. (1974). Practical aspects of field research. *Clinical Social Work Journal, 2*(3), 182-193.

Wodarski, J. S., Thyer, B. A., Iodice, J. D., & Pinkston, R. H. (1991). Graduate social work education: A review of empirical research. *Journal of Social Service Research, 14*, 23-44.

Wodarski, J. S. & Wodarski, L. A. (in press). *Curriculums and practical aspects of implementation: Preventive health services for adolescents.* Lanham, Maryland: University Press of America.

Chapter 3

Social Group Work, Sink or Swim: Where Is Group in a Generalist Curriculum?

Joan K. Parry

Where is social work with groups today? I believe this to be a rhetorical question, since we all have an anecdotal feeling that group work is an increased modality for almost every type of service agency in the community. However, whether or not this proliferation of groups is *social work* with groups is the important question. When the intervention is conceptualized and understood as group therapy, the intervention removes itself from the arena of social work. Group therapy is directed to middle-class adults and, as Middleman and Goldberg-Wood (1990) state, cannot be considered social work, although therapy can be the content of social work with groups. In addition, the notion of the power of diversity is far beyond that of therapy.

It is important to understand the relevance of the group for practice in all social work methods and in multiple settings and varied situations. Individuals live and relate in groups: primary, work, religious, and leisure groups. Families are groups, and community workers must be knowledgeable in groups to provide meaningful help. The supervisor/administrator will be more effective in committees, task groups, staff meetings, and at board meetings if the person is skilled in work with groups.

HISTORY

From where has social work with groups come? Social reform and social justice were the main themes from which work with groups emerged. Today we are still struggling to keep the ideas of social justice and reform in the forefront of local, state, and national debate. Breton says if our actions do not reflect our concerns for social justice, we are irrelevant to the poor, the oppressed, the minorities, and the marginalized (1990, p. 25). Gertrude Wilson (1976) discussed the YMCAs and YWCAs which were introduced into the United States in 1866 from London. The focus of the groups in these agencies was to promote the mental, moral, physical, social, and spiritual welfare of youth (1976, pg. 6). The concerns of group workers in this early period were poverty, low wages, working hours, and poor housing, as well as caste-class treatment of people (Wilson, 1976).

By the mid-1920s, the group had become one of the more important modalities of service. To be a social group worker was a legitimate role. Social reform and social justice were a mandate to the social group worker. Group work as part of academe occurred in the following decade of the 1930s and is discussed by Coyle (1947). Throughout the 1940s and 1950s, group was one of the modalities used in hospitals, family and children's agencies, public welfare, correctional facilities, psychiatric clinics, public schools, and recreation settings.

ACADEME

In academe, practice curriculum was conceptualized as casework, group work, and community organization. This practice curriculum was in effect in schools of social work from post-World War II to the early 1960s. Group work was swimming strongly in tandem with its methodology siblings, casework, and community organization. NASW, the professional association, was established in 1955 with leaders from all three methods in practice and academe. The Committee on Practice of Group work section was originally chaired by Ruby Pernell, followed by Helen Northen and then Miriam Cohen. But the group work section of NASW was abolished in 1963 (Wilson, 1976).

A similar trend was occurring in social work education. The reorganization of the American Association of Schools of Social Work into the Council on Social Work Education occurred in 1952. Schwartz called this development a unifying trend in social work and said it pushed schools of social work to look for a common frame of reference. He suggested group workers were pressed to dig deeply for their social work connections and identify their contribution to a larger definition of social work practice, of which work with groups would be but a special case (1977). In the late 1960s and the 1970s social work with groups began to sink. This was occurring despite the proliferation of groups in the service arena. Academe was giving up its responsibility to educate for practice in the headlong search for the generic method.

Academe, for the most part, was changing its curriculum from separate practice methodologies to the generic/generalist conceptualization. During this period, Perlman noted this trend and stated, ". . . group work is increasingly overlapping with the casework method" (1965, p. 171). To reiterate, there were diverse forces pushing toward the idea that social work practice is inclusive, and a division by methodology was not a good way of describing social work practice. Reynolds said, "The lines between casework and group began to waver" (1965, p. 7). During the period when schools of social work conferred a degree in group work, students were required to have a certain minimum of courses in casework. Unfortunately, no course in group was required for students who graduated with a casework major (Reynolds, 1965). In such a climate, group work began to sink. In fact, Hartford (1978, p. 12) commented that "we are lessening the amount of knowledge we are teaching about small groups . . . just at the moment when we are expecting all social workers should be able to use group methods."

Group workers were always a considerably smaller number than those who perceived themselves as caseworkers/psychotherapists.

Even during the period of group work as a method in academe and as a legitimate professional identity in the service arena, group work was swimming upstream. Because the number of educated group workers was small even at its height of acceptance, psychiatrists were recruited to work with groups. Many times, social work interns become cofacilitators in groups with other professionals. This type of service is known as group therapy. Middleman and Goldberg-Wood point out the appeal of the word "therapy." It often equates with high status. Therapy connects workers and students to psychiatrists/psychologists and disconnects them from the social welfare arena and the poor (Middleman & Goldberg-Wood, 1990, p. 9).

GENERALIST CURRICULUM

As the generalist curriculum became a reality in schools of social work in the decade of the 1980s, group work was struggling to keep its head above water. The generalist curriculum claims that practice courses teach about work with individuals, family, and group dynamics. Is social work with groups in that package? Again, perhaps a rhetorical question. Gitterman and Germain suggested that professional streams of thought tend to dichotomize social action/environmental change (cause) and an individualized method of helping people with needs and problems (function). In addition, they stated that support of one over the other tends to polarize the profession (1981, p. 45). Social work with groups is an effective way to integrate cause and function.

Another dichotomy is the macro-micro conceptualization. Micro is conceived as practice with individuals, families, and groups. Macro is practice with organizations and communities. Again, social work with groups bridges this dichotomy. Social work with groups includes personal problems for members, enhancement for members, work with boards and committees, task groups, etc.

A study conducted with practice faculty at schools of social work found that 77% of respondents defined their own views of social work practice as coming close to a comprehensive definition which covered a full range of both micro and macro social work practice. However, these same respondents did not conceptualize their own teaching in this comprehensive way. In this particular group of respondents, 86% specified casework as the area in which they were most adequately prepared; 10% of respondents reported being most prepared in group work, while only 4% indicated being most prepared in community organization (Bakalinsky, 1982).

Another study of generalist practice suggested that the generalist practitioner has knowledge and understanding of varying methods of intervention such as family treatment, short-term treatment, and group treatment (Teigiser, 1983). The idea of *treatment* itself is antithetical to social work with groups. Social work practice is once again equated with therapy and disconnected from its roots, that of working with the poor and disenfranchised. Shapiro (1990) comments that group work provides a multidimensional arena in which members encounter one another's frames of reference. Social work with groups combines wisdom and experience in working toward more fulfilling transactions between the individual, the small group, and the community (Breton, 1990). Group *treatment* does not suggest a rich tradition, imbued with the strains of social reform and social justice.

Teigiser summarizes the study of generalist student graduates with social treatment graduates by finding that generalist graduates more often practiced at larger system levels, i.e., macro practice. Teigiser also stated that demands on "social workers require them to assume roles beyond those of clinician, administrator, researcher, or policy analyst" (1983, p. 84). What concerns me is the role of the clinician. Who is a clinical social worker? Is the clinical social worker the psychotherapist in sheep's clothing? Social work with groups is drowning under the term clinical social worker. Middleman (1990, plenary address) says the profession's (NASW) priority has moved from social change and environmental concerns to the term "clinical."

Another dichotomy is the idea that social work practice can be split into direct and indirect practice. LeCroy and Goodwin (1988) provided a content analysis of course outlines in their article. The course outlines are from those faculty who are teaching methods. Their study represents 65% of the MSW programs in the United States. Methods are conceptualized as direct practice. The most frequently covered unit reported from course outlines was "treatment" process. In addition, most of the respondents' course outlines covered were introductory materials, the social work relationship, and assessment. The study lists five other course units such as ethnic-sensitive practice, crisis intervention, and termination. There is no mention of social work with groups.

It is extremely difficult to locate groups or group work in the generalist curriculum. The course content listed above could also be content that could be found in a course on social work with groups, but the idea of group is well hidden. All of the above discourse suggests the reasons for the start-up of the new journal, *Social Work with Groups,* which began in 1978 with Papell and Rothman as the founding editors. This was quickly followed by the formation of the Association for the Advancement of Social Work with Groups (AASWG) in 1979. Both the Journal and the AASWG met a pent-up demand for a forum to share group work knowledge and skills. I am talking to you from the podium of the Thirteenth Annual Symposium of AASWG. Through all these years, volunteers who cared deeply about groups made a symposium possible. We became a membership organization a few years ago and continue to grow. Still, I feel very much in agreement with Middleman's comment at her plenary speech at the Twelfth Symposium that "we have talked mainly to ourselves" (1990).

OTHER ROLES FOR THE SOCIAL GROUP WORKER

It is time for those of us who care about groups to speak out. We need to speak out beyond the group work family, to those who do not understand the power of groups, to those who are unaware of how closely social work with groups is integrated with individual work, family work, community work, and administrative work. It is also important that we speak out about how it is possible to capture the power of diversity through service in groups. This diversity is demonstrated in a study of social work with groups in which the study suggests multiple roles for the group worker. The worker moves from a therapeutic and individually oriented role in a personal change group to a teacher or facilitator role in a developmental group, and in social change groups, the worker takes on a consultation role (Paquet-Deehy et al., 1985).

Consultation is a role to which social group workers must give more time and effort. In this role, those of us who are committed to groups must teach field instructors, colleagues, and agency administrators the way to use groups for serving clients, as well as using group concepts and group skills to work with committees, boards, funding sources, etc. The basic group work elements of size, composition, membership, leadership, collaboration, conflict, role distribution, power, authority, intimacy, and developmental stages are experienced collectively in a staff group, a board, or another type of work group, according to Brown (1988). The group consultant's role can be in-house or external. The focus of the work must have clarity of purpose, and the methods can vary from a direct training method to participant involvement in the group. Thus, social work with groups through the consultation model can involve people with power to make change for those people who have no power.

An important value of social work with groups is that of participatory democracy and citizenship building. These are concepts which, by their very nature, are group centered. Settlement leaders were devoted to democratic group processes to develop responsible citizenship (Gitterman, 1981). Groups suggest themes of shared control and shared power. Schwartz (1985/86) talked about leadership which brings the joys of collaboration rather than the action of the knower on the naive, the strong on the weak, the expert on the uninitiated. As people feel comfortable in being together in a group and are able to share, be open, risk, and lend a hand to another, they begin to feel the sense of groupness, the sense of the power of the collective strength, and the sense of a shared process. Since collective action has greater visibility, the group becomes a powerful force for social influence and organizational change (Gitterman, 1986, p. 32).

SUMMARY

Thus, we can see that the generic/generalist curriculum may describe itself as macro-micro, direct-indirect, integrated, foundation, individual-family-group, clinical-nonclinical, multi-method, and other such labels. This hodgepodge of ideas has not brought clarity to social work practice and has all but sunk social work with groups. This melange of ideas about social work practice has become an attempt to capture the essence of social work and has, in fact, become a maelstrom in which the individual pieces are struggling to extricate themselves; in particular, social work with groups. Lee has commented that the union of social group work with social work has meant some loss of identity, since group work had not quite consolidated its own identity before joining social work. Group work, therefore, needs to continue to identify its distinct contributions and hold on to its uniqueness more than it has (1985/86, p. 40).

And finally, does group work exist in a generalist curriculum in which the "helping process" is taught? When social work educators teach about beginnings, are the tasks the same for the social worker with individuals, families, and groups? Is contracting, assessment, intervention the same for the social worker with individuals, families, and groups? Gitterman commented that in the beginning stage there is a particular body of knowledge distinctive to group, and it requires special emphasis, such as "the process of *forming* a group and *proffering* a service" (1981, p. 71). He continued by noting all the factors we know are required: clarity of purpose, composition, size, time, place, and so on. Thus, although there are similarities for educators when teaching a generalist/integrative approach to helping in the classroom, the differences are evident. The body of knowledge about group work does not easily fit into a generalist curriculum. I feel that confining group work content to just one semester is a bind on the educator. I raised multiple questions in a previous article about teaching group work in one semester: What is essential knowledge? What is the best way to get across the "how to's"? How many theoretical models can be included? How best can students be helped to understand the many forms group work can take in working with people? (Parry, 1988, p. 78).

Social work with groups has developed skills which have influenced the whole profession; i.e., skills of working with media, the arts, non-verbal, games, and so on. Many of these skills can be used with adults who are distressed and cannot easily express themselves. The informal approach has been a valuable tool in working with suspicious and hostile people. Social work with groups fulfills the mandate of the profession to serve minorities, to serve vulnerable populations, and to provide enhancement/enrichment services to clients/members who are working together in a democratic process.

Thus, we must all take up the mantle and spread our knowledge/ skills of social work with groups to our agencies, our schools, and our colleagues. Let's help group work swim back into the mainstream of social work education and practice.

REFERENCES

Bakalinsky, R. (1982). Generic practice in graduate social work curriculum: A study of educators' experiences and attitudes. *Journal of Education for Social Work, 18*(3), 46-54.

Breton, M. (1990). Learning from social group work traditions. *Social Work with Groups, 13*(3), 21-34.

Brown, A. (1988). Consultation for groupworkers: Models and methods. *Social Work with Groups, 11*(1/2), 145-163.

Coyle, G. L. (1947). *Group experience and democratic values.* New York: Women's Press.

Gitterman, A. (1985/86). The group work tradition and social work practice. *Social Work with Groups, 8*(4), 39-50.

Gitterman, A. (1981). Group work content in an integrated method curriculum. In Sonia Leib Abels & Paul Abels (Eds.). *Proceedings: 1979 Symposium, Social Work with Groups.* Louisville, Kentucky: Association for the Advancement of Social Work With Groups.

Gitterman, A., & Germain, C. B. (1981). Education for practice: Teaching about the environment. *Journal of Education for Social Work, 17*(3), 44-51.

Hartford, M. E. (1978). Groups in the human services: Some facts and fancies. *Social Work with Groups, 1*(1), 7-13.

LeCroy, C. W., & Goodwin, C. C. (1988). New directions in teaching social work methods: A content analysis of course outlines. *Journal of Social Work Education, 24*(1), 43-49.

Lee, J. A. B. (1985/86). Seeing it whole: Social work with groups within an integrative perspective. *Social Work with Groups, 8*(4), 39-50.

Middleman, R. R. (1990). Group work and the Heimlich maneuver: Unchoking social work education. Plenary Address, Twelfth (12) Symposium, Association for the Advancement of Social Work with Groups, Miami, Florida. October 28, 1990.

Middleman, R. R., & Wood, G. G. (1990). From social group work to social work with groups. *Social Work with Groups, 13*(3), 3-20.

Paquet-Deehy, A., Hopmeyer, E., Home, A., and Kislowicz, L. (1985). A typology of social work practice with groups. *Social Work with Groups, 8*(1), 65-78.

Parry, J. K. (1988). Organizing principles for developing a foundation group work practice course. *Social Work with Groups, 11*(1/2), 77-85.

Perlman, H. H. (1965). Social work method: A review of the past decade. *Social Work, 10*(4), 166-178.

Reynolds, B. C. (1965). *Learning and teaching in the practice of social work.* Silver Spring, MD: NASW Classics Edition.

Schwartz, W. (1985/86). The group work tradition and social work practice. *Social Work with Groups, 8*(4), 7-27.

Schwartz, W. (1977). Social group work: The interactionist approach. *Encyclopedia of Social Work,* 17th Issue, Vol. 2. Washington, DC: NASW.

Shapiro, B. Z. (1990). The Social Work Group as Social Work Microcosum: Frames of Reference Revisited. *Social Work with Groups. 13*(2), pp. 5-21.

Teigiser, K. S. (1983). Evaluation of education for generalist practice. *Journal of Education for Social Work, 19*(1), 79-85.

Wilson, G. (1976). From practice to theory: A personalized history. In R. W. Roberts & Helen Northen (Eds.). *Theories of social work with groups.* New York: Columbia University Press.

Chapter 4

The Crisis of Diversity

Larry E. Davis

Colleagues and friends, it is with both honor and pride that I speak with you this morning. It seems for me that life has come full circle. So many of you here have been my professors and mentors, and so many others my colleagues and friends. I am truly pleased to have the opportunity to attempt to give back something to a group of professionals who have contributed so much to my own personal academic growth and development.

I still remember quite clearly how I got into group work–by mistake!!

Upon being accepted to the University of Michigan's School of Social Work I was asked to inform my advisor as to what I wanted to study. I proceeded to describe to him what I now realize is Community Organization.

However, being a good social worker he understood my naive description of what I said I wanted to do and concluded with the comment, "Oh yes, you'll love group work."

After having been so well understood and wisely advised, I began to take group work courses. I took courses from Charles Garvin, Frank Maple, Charles Wolfson, Harvey Bertcher, Rose Mary Sarri, Robert Vinter, Sally Churchill, and Paul Glasser.

As you can see the errors of my education were numerous. Yet my advisor in his unwitting, but prophetic wisdom, was correct; I do love group work. And fortunately for me the teachings of my professors have been long lasting.

However, since I took my first group work course in 1968 much has happened to change our society. America is experiencing a demographic crisis. Both race and class are increasing rather than decreasing in their levels of importance. This fact is probably both surprising and disappointing to those of you who participated in the civil and social struggles of the 1960s, 1970s, and 1980s. An increase in the importance of race and class factors is surprising because so much progress appeared to have been made, and disappointing because it appears that there is so much which remains unfinished.

Unquestionably the current racial and class crisis is at odds with the aspirations of group work professionals both white and minority, most of whom had worked for and anticipated a diminution in the societal importance of race and class as predictors of life events. Unfortunately, this is not the case. It is apparent that both of these demographics will have profound social and political implications for the rest of our professional lives.

Why is this so? Let us address first, the racial factor.

A number of factors have contributed to sustaining race as a major issue for group work professionals. Foremost, the numbers of minorities are growing faster than that of whites, thereby increasing the numbers of probable multiracial group work situations. For example, from 1980 to 1990 the total U.S. population grew by 9.8% from approximately 224 million to 249 million. However, the Asian population (now 7.3 million) grew by 107%, Native Americans (now 2 million) grew by 38%, blacks (now 30 million) grew by 13%, and Hispanics (now 22.4 million) grew by 53%. In 1980 one in five Americans belonged to one of these groups, now one in four does. At the same time, despite the increasing numbers of minority members in our society, they continue to be largely segregated from whites and from the opportunities of mainstream America. This fact has served to foster continued mistrust and misunderstanding between whites and nonwhites.

Secondly, the importance of social class in our society has become increasingly obvious to all who are paying even slight attention. Indeed, economic issues have become progressively important as large segments of our society have become impoverished. Our society has in the last decade moved with deliberate speed toward a society of have and have nots. At present nearly 70% of the country's wealth is controlled by 10% of the population. These shifts in our society's income distributions have been nothing short of dramatic. For example, since the late 1970s the income of the top one-fifth of American families has increased by 18% while the bottom one-fifth has seen a decrease in income of 5%. At the same time, the incomes of the richest 1% have doubled during this period.

Furthermore, our society relative to other industrialized nations such as Canada, Britain, West Germany, Italy, and Sweden, seems unwilling or unable to alter the scourge of poverty. For example, in comparison to the countries noted above, poverty in America is more widespread and severe, poor families stay poor longer, and our programs are least effective in lifting families and poor children out of poverty.

This increasing racial and class diversification within our society portends that there will be more minority and poor clients needing professional social work services. However, the largely middle income white professionals who will be asked to help them will often have had little prior contact with minorities and the poor, and hence probably little substantive knowledge about them. At the same time, minorities and the poor are apt to become increasingly distrustful of "group leaders from a system" which has become less sensitive and responsive to their needs. Resultingly we are left with a worst-case scenario: growing numbers of minority clients who must be helped largely by whites, and growing numbers of poor clients who must be helped largely by members of the middle class. In both of these instances, group workers are apt to understand too little about their group members, and the group members are apt to have too little trust in those on whom they must rely to lead them.

It is with this diversifying race/class scenario in mind that I make this address. For despite the difficulty and the seeming unmanageableness of this crisis it will be group work professionals like yourselves who will be called into service, and it is from you that much will be expected.

I would like to share with you what I believe will be some of the major concerns of minority and poor group members as they seek our assistance. And lastly I shall suggest what some of our responses as group workers might be. However, let me first offer just a little backdrop on race and class as practice issues.

RACE RELATIONS AND CROSS-RACIAL PRACTICE

The importance of race as a practice issue in social work was largely ignored until the 1960s. Before then our profession had engaged in what was thought to be "color-blind practice": that is, to ignore the color or racial identity of our clients. This strategy I believe was not ill intended, but was adapted as an attempt to reduce practitioner "racial bias." For during this time the helping professions equated the acknowledgement of racial differences with racism. Theoretically, at least, color-blind practice ("treating everyone the same") was an attempt to "control" for client-worker racial differences. However, it also served to allow the practitioner and client (mainly the practitioner) an opportunity to avoid both the cognitive and effective components of America's legacy of racial turmoil. In retrospect, it now seems obvious to most of us that a strategy which attempted to ignore so much of what was central to the client would greatly restrain the helping relationship. It simultaneously limited questions which the leader might need ask, and disclosures which the group members might need make.

A brief perusal of the race relations literature makes it apparent that two major social dynamics have contributed to making the cross-racial practice experience problematic: A history of racial conflict and discrimination, coupled with continued racial segregation.

For example, even the most recent studies in race relations suggest that there are significant differences in the life experiences of whites and nonwhites. Perhaps some of you saw the recent ABC-TV *Prime Time Live*. St. Louis was selected for the study because it was a middle-American city not known for any racial crisis at the time.

They had two 28-year-old men, one black and one white, with similar incomes and educations to present themselves in a variety of social situations. The black man, when inquiring about an apartment, was told that someone had already put money down on it, while his white counterpart was told that the unit was immediately available. When inquiring about a help-wanted sign posted in a dry cleaner's window, the black man was told that the position was already taken, but his white counterpart was told that the job was available. When they inquired about purchasing a car at a local dealership, the black male was quoted both a higher price and interest rate than that of his white counterpart.

Such differences in the life experiences of whites and nonwhites do not make our jobs as cross-racial helpers easier. We would be naive, indeed, if we believed that our clients are unaware of such racial realities.

Neither group leaders nor their members are oblivious to this social political history. On the contrary, it is because both are aware of this legacy that neither may be comfortable initiating a discussion on race. In this sense both leaders and members may be reluctant to acknowledge race as an issue for fear of arousing anger or ill will in the other. In particular, minority clients may fear renewed racial rejection from a group leader who is white, and white members may fear some form of racial retaliation from group leaders who are minorities. Subsequently, it is often the case that neither whites nor minorities trust the other sufficiently to allow for the establishment of open group communication.

At the same time, racial segregation in employment and housing, although no longer legal, is still more the rule than the exception. Hence not only are cross-racial leader/ member interactions hampered by the past, but also by the present. Whites and minorities continue largely to go to different schools, live in different neighborhoods, attend different churches, and socialize in different parts of the city. As a consequence of this continued separation of the races, they often know very little about the social realities of the other. Indeed, the pervasiveness of the racial segregation of whites and minorities has frequently resulted in white leaders commonly having had almost no meaningful contact with minorities before seeing them as members in his or her group. The separation of whites and minorities is so complete as to result in their possessing often contrary and conflicting views of the world. Not surprisingly they are often said to live in different worlds, and to subsequently possess different world views.

Of course, a variety of educational efforts on the part of social work educators have been undertaken to include content on minorities into the group work experiences of social work students. But as most of us are aware, this information is often superficial and academic, and sometimes reluctantly taught by those who must teach it. At the same time, it is difficult even with the best instruction and with the best intentions to acquire knowledge about the cultural nuances of a people in the absence of meaningful interactions with them.

Before moving on I will make just a few comments on "Class as a practice issue."

No other profession is so characterized by the delivery of services by one social class of people to another, as is social work. Yet despite our professional mandate to help the poor it has become clear to me that group workers, indeed helping professions as a whole, actually know very little about class as a dynamic that effects group processes. With respect to understanding behavior, most of what we attribute to class is probably better explained by the absence of opportunity. This fact became very apparent to me during my efforts to write a chapter on class and group work practice. The absence of our knowledge in this area is impressive. However, it seems to me that at least part of our ignorance on this topic can be traced to our reliance on college students for small group experimentation. For, unlike the variables of race and gender there tends to be comparatively little class heterogeneity on college campuses, from whence most experimental subjects are drawn.

However, presently, our understanding of class is bolstered by our understanding of status. Fortunately, we do know a fair amount about the effects of status expectations on behavior: Hopefully, what little is known can be successfully transferred to our work with groups.

IMPLICATIONS FOR PRACTICE

So, where do we go from here? What have theory, research, and practice wisdom to offer us in the face of working with populations who promise to be increasingly different from ourselves? What major concerns confront us, and how might we as group work professionals respond to these concerns?

The source of concern for us as group work practitioners is apt to come from what can be called the "phenomena of difference." It seems that a visual difference of any sort results in the viewer assuming that the perceived difference is but a reflection of other underlying differences as well. In other words, a perceived difference in skin color or social status is thought to reflect a difference in thinking and feeling about the world–needless to say this is often the case.

The perception of a racial or class difference between ourselves and our group members is apt to result in their asking three questions about us:

1. Are we people of goodwill?
2. Do we have sufficient mastery/skills to help them?
3. Do we understand their social realities?

Let me respond to these questions.

Goodwill

Are we people of goodwill? Do we mean them harm? Do we have their best interests at heart? These are reasonable questions to ask of anyone whom we view as different from ourselves. Most minority or poor clients are apt to think, even if they don't ask, "Does this group leader dislike people like me? Is he or she biased against Asians, Hispanics, black, or Native Americans?" Or, is he or she classist, that is, biased against poor women or children (who by the way make up 70% of those who are poor in America)? Do they perceive me as a "welfare cheat, or just one of those truly greedy types?"

Fortunately, social group workers tend to have a good image in this respect. It will probably not be too hard to convince your group members that you are on their side. And there is a potential word of good news for white group workers. The research in this area suggests that minorities tend to distrust "those other white" therapists, but find "their own white" therapists to be okay. So, while this is probably the first question which enters the mind of minority or poor group members, upon your initial interaction with them, it is a question to which most of you should have little problem in finding the right answers. However, I do believe that this question will typically be of greater concern to white than to minority group leaders, and to men more than to women. (Women are typically viewed as being less aggressive and minorities less powerful.)

Mastery

Once you have managed to convince your different race/class group members that you are not their adversary, you are likely to be confronted with another question. Do you have sufficient mastery or skills to be of help? In other words, are you professionally capable of assisting them with their problems? Most of you will be able to easily put such fears to rest by merely pointing to your credentials on the wall. But for others of you, namely minorities (and to a lesser extent females), your competence as a group leader will likely be questioned subtly, if not overtly. Some members may ask you such things as, "Have you been doing this kind of work long?" or "Where did you go to school?" Or the most painful of such questions, "Where is the real group leader today?" Again, most of you will survive this brief inquisition, but it is always painful, especially for those minorities and women whose professional competence is so frequently questioned. Finally, consider the following question.

Do We Understand the Client's Social Reality?

I do not want to suggest that the questions of goodwill and mastery are not important as they are, but it is this final question which is most critical in cross-racial cross-class helping situations.

The concern likely to be experienced by group members once perceiving a racial or class difference is whether the different race or class helper understands their world sufficiently to be of assistance to them. The client may wonder, "Does the practitioner have sufficient knowledge of the world which I see and experience to be of any real help to me?" This is a question which many clients are likely to think, even if they fail to ask. Having an adequate understanding of the client's social reality or world view has been identified to be among the most critical of practice issues.

Different race/class group members may suspect that a given group leader has had little or no prior experience interacting with members of their minority group or social class. Unfortunately, their fears are often confirmed. For example, minority members are likely to say to themselves, "Yes, my group leader is a person of goodwill." That is, he or she is a well-meaning person and is genuinely trying to assist me with my difficulties. And yes, he or she is sufficiently trained and skilled as a practitioner–just look at those degrees on the wall and the job position that he or she holds. But even though this practitioner means well, and is well educated, what does he or she know about being Asian, black, Hispanic, Native American, or poor? Such concerns on the behalf of minority and poor clients are what I call "healthy skepticism." In other words, the client does not feel that the group leader means them harm, but rather questions whether the leader will, because of his or her lack of knowledge about them, be able to "do them any good."

Not surprisingly, most groups leaders may attempt to hide the fact that they are often ignorant about the culture, values, norms, and the language of their different race/class group members. Such attempts are, however, likely to become problematic as most group members are soon likely to realize that their dissimilar group leader is only pretending to understand them. The member may soon ask, is the leader also only pretending to be a person of goodwill?

A COURSE OF ACTION–WHAT SHOULD WE DO?

In view of the increasing probability of leader/member racial and class differences and the importance of these differences to practice, you are probably asking: "So Davis, what suggestions do you have to offer us?"

Well, most certainly I do not come with all the answers to what will surely be awkward and difficult moments ahead for all of us. But neither have I come completely empty-handed. Let me offer the following suggestions: First, we must continue to remind ourselves that behavior is purposive or purposeful. The extent to which we see the behavior of our group members as being meaningful rather than foolish or stupid, the greater will be our ability to assist them. I firmly believe that this is the most important factor to keep in mind when working with populations with whom we have little prior knowledge. In such instances we must assume that the behaviors we observe make sense given the realities our clients face. Rarely do people engage in nonsensical behavior. In general, people attempt to make life better for themselves and rarely do whole groups, strata, or classes of people simultaneously go crazy.

Second, we must make every effort in our work with minorities and the poor to demonstrate respect. The demonstration of respect is imperative when working with those whom society often holds in low esteem. Especially upon the initial meeting, avoid professional shortcuts and informalities. In other words, don't cut corners with those whom society is cutting short.

Third, we must spend some time examining our own attitudes and beliefs regarding those clients who differ from us so as to make our attitudes and beliefs more sensitive and appropriate. It has been suggested that the most dangerous thing about myths is that we assume them to be true.

The inspection of our attitudes and beliefs regarding a particular racial/class group is perhaps best done in some form of consultation with members or perhaps colleagues who belong to the group with which we plan to work. Here I offer a special plea to minorities: you have colleagues who need assistance in working with a given minority population. Your failure to assist your colleagues will later only result in their failure to assist their clients.

Fourth, we must develop a wide repertoire of helping skills. That is, we must employ group means of intervention which are culturally and class appropriate. If you need assistance in enhancing your group skills pick up a copy of *Race, Gender, and Class.* You should find it useful.

Fifth, we must be knowledgeable of resources which exist in the larger society, not just within our particular agencies or settings. For example, church leaders, spiritual healers, and extended family members may prove very instrumental to your intervention efforts.

Sixth, we must attempt to get off to a good start. Some have found that as many as 70% of minority clients fail to return to our offices following their first visit. Our initial contacts with those who differ from us are likely to be our most important, perhaps our only chance to establish a positive rapport with these clients.

Seventh, we must anticipate success. While the client-therapist dissimilarity has the potential to be problematic, it need not be. We can, by our expectations, serve to create positive self-fulfilling prophecies for our group members. We must believe in our skills and in our group members abilities to achieve successful outcomes.

Some of you are perhaps aware that the Chinese characters for "crisis" and "opportunity" are the same. The current demographic crisis affords group workers with a tremendous opportunity to assist in helping America accommodate this crisis.

However, before concluding let me address one final concern. There are some who might ask why don't we just have whites lead groups of whites and minorities lead groups of minorities?

And still others would say that the poor should only be helped by others who are themselves poor. To such arguments I offer the following expression. "Reality will tolerate fantasy, but will not spare it." By this I mean that whether I like it or not, or whether you like it nor not, and to a great extent whether those who need help like it or not, minorities will continue to be assigned to whites as group members. And the poor will continue to be seen largely by leaders who are middle class.

Hence my colleagues and friends, the question which faces us as helping professionals is not *will* but *whether*. The question is not: Will group members of color be seen by white group leaders? Or will the poor be seen by professionals who are members of the middle class? No, the question is whether.

Whether we as different race/class group workers will be sufficiently skilled, knowledgeable, and sensitive to the issues of diversity to lead our groups effectively.

Best wishes to you all.

Chapter 5

Building
an Empirical Foundation
for Social Work with Groups

Rowena Grice Wilson
Alvin Walter

The empirical practice movement represents a significant development within the profession of social work that holds promise for contributing to the construction of an empirical base for social work practice with groups. Empirical practice refers to the utilization of scientific research to generate knowledge and technology relevant to broad professional purposes and to immediate practice operations (Reid & Smith, 1981). Empirical practice also refers to a style of practice (Reid, 1987) which is characteristic of the clinician-researcher (Jayaratne & Levy, 1979), clinical scientist (Briar, 1977), and the practitioner-researcher (Wood, 1980). The notion of empirical practice not only provides a framework for the integration of practice and research at the practitioner level, but can be utilized as a framework for the generation of knowledge in all areas of social work practice.

HISTORICAL OVERVIEW

The utility of research for the development of knowledge for practice has been the focus of the writings of prominent social workers and social work researchers such as Mary Richmond (1917), Maurice Karpf (1931), Margaret Blenkner (1950), David French (1952), and many others. Historical themes and landmark developments which illuminate the profession's long-standing commitment to the development of scientific knowledge for practice have been provided by Zimbalist (1977) and others (Austin, 1991; Fanshel, 1980; Maas, 1977; MacDonald, 1960; Polansky, 1971; Reid, 1983, 1987; Tripodi, 1984). These reports also chronicle the slow but steady accumulation of research undertaken by social workers in all areas of practice over the years.

The role of research in social work and the question, "How scientific is social work?" are perennial issues that have been the focus of articles, master's theses, and books published early in the history of organized social work (Deutschberger, 1948; Gordon, 1952, 1958; Greenwood, 1957; Kahn, 1954; Karpf, 1931; Social Work Research Group, 1955). These issues continue to be addressed in contemporary social work literature (Dean, 1989; Dean & Fenby, 1989; Fischer, 1981, 1984; Gordon, 1983; Hartman, 1990; Heineman-Pieper, 1988; Imre, 1984; Ivanoff & Blythe, 1989; Ivanoff, Blythe, & Briar, 1987; Karger, 1983; Peile, 1988; Schuerman, 1987; Thyer, 1989; Witkin, 1991; Wood, 1990). The persistent concern about the social work knowledge base is responsible, in part, for the emergence of the empirical practice movement and the development of the empirical clinical practice model.

Empirical Practice

Empirical practice, as defined by Siegel (1984), emphasizes the following attributes of the social work practitioner who engages in empirically based practice:

1. makes maximum use of research findings,
2. collects data systematically to monitor the intervention,
3. demonstrates empirically whether or not interventions are effective,
4. specifies problems, interventions, and outcomes in terms that are concrete, observable, and measurable,
5. uses research ways of thinking and research methods in defining clients' problems, formulating questions for practice, col-

lecting assessment data, evaluating the effectiveness of interventions, and using evidence,

6. views research and practice as a part of the same problem-solving process, and
7. views research as a tool to be used in practice (p. 329).

The use of the empirical orientation to practice is considered to be one way of integrating research and practice at the practitioner level. Some writers also believe that the knowledge derived from testing practice hypotheses at times will articulate with larger scale research on practice and in the behavioral sciences (Glasser & Garvin, 1976).

DEVELOPMENT AND UTILIZATION OF EMPIRICAL KNOWLEDGE IN SOCIAL WORK

Efforts to construct a scientific knowledge base for social work practice have not achieved the results anticipated by the pioneers (Reid, 1987). Moreover, the promise of empirical practice, as envisioned over a decade ago, has yet to be realized (Briar, 1990). Practitioners are not likely to engage in research or to utilize research to guide practice (Kirk, 1979, 1990; Richey, Blythe, & Berlin, 1987; Rosen & Mutschler, 1982; Rosenblatt, 1968). Furthermore, education in the empirical practice perspective seems to have had a limited impact on the profession, thus far (Briar, 1990).

Reasons offered for the limited utilization of research by practitioners include the possibility that social workers do not find research knowledge useful in solving practice problems (LeCroy, 1990; Rosenblatt, 1968). Ashford and LeCroy (1991), argue that working knowledge and practice wisdom are utilized most often by social workers because these sources of information are sufficient to resolve immediate practice situations. LeCroy (1990) argues for a broader conceptualization of knowledge that recognizes the existence of a "continuum of knowledge" that is available to inform practice. The integration of research and practice was viewed as a complex process that affects research utilization by practitioners. LeCroy suggests that the key to enhancing research utilization is an understanding of how social workers use knowledge.

Another reason for the limited utilization of research by practitioners may be related to dissemination. Shilling (1990) suggests that research findings be disseminated through workshops, following a "design-and-development approach" that will bring packaged interventions to workers. Involvement of administrators and practicum field instructors was also suggested as a means to increase utilization by students and practitioners within the field context.

Much needs to be accomplished with regard to knowledge development and research utilization within the profession. This is particularly true for social work practice with groups.

RESEARCH ON SOCIAL WORK PRACTICE WITH GROUPS

There has been increased attention directed toward the development of practitioner-researchers and research-practitioner career specialists in social work (Austin, 1991; Bloom & Fischer, 1982; Jayaratne & Levy, 1979; Reid & Smith, 1981). Moreover, the inaugural issues of Research on Social Work Practice (Thyer, 1991) exemplifies the extent of professional commitment to the content and application of the scientific method to practice, and punctuates the steady movement in this regard. Notwithstanding these developments, there is a serious paucity of group work research and published reports about empirical clinical practice with groups (Feldman, 1987; Northen, 1989; Silverman, 1966; Rothman & Fike, 1987; Russell, 1990).

Knowledge About Social Work with Groups

Consistent with trends in the profession as a whole, social group work practice has an established tradition of the use of research as one of the important means for developing practice knowledge. On the basis of an analysis of the similarities and differences in ten models of group work practice, Northen and Roberts (1976) examined the status of practice theory related to social work with groups. They pointed out that social work with groups had "an early and continuing commitment to research on [group] *process and outcome*" (p. 368). Important landmarks in the development of group work practice theory were identified as seminal studies and research undertakings by pioneers such as Kaiser (1930), Coyle (1930), and Newstetter (1947). Thus, the current movement toward the development of a scientific knowledge base for social work practice with groups can be linked to the 1930s, a period of formulation and organization of group work as a method of social work practice (Alissi, 1980).

Basic assumptions about social group work practice. The knowledge base of social group work practice rests on some basic assumptions about (1) the significance of group experiences to individuals and (2) the role of the social worker (Coyle, 1980). A basic assumption is that group experiences are beneficial to individuals in a variety of ways, but also may have negative effects on some individuals (Galinsky & Schopler, 1977; Kaiser, 1980; Levinson, 1973; Northen, 1987). Another basic assumption is that group work is unique and therefore fundamentally different from group therapies in other professions (Lang, 1979). These differences relate to ". . . the view of the individual, the conception and use of the group, the perspective of the change mechanism, and the perception of the professional role and tasks" (p. 271). Thus, the social group work practitioner needs professional education in social work and must possess specialized knowledge and skills about group processes and methods of practice with various types of groups (Coyle, 1980).

Conceptual framework of social group work. In 1958, Clara Kaiser (1980) identified three categories of concepts pertinent to group work practice: (1) values and goals, (2) group processes, and (3) methodology (methods and techniques of the social group work process). Value concepts were viewed as fundamentally the social work value base. Goal concepts referred to concepts related to (a) the dual focus of goals on the individual and the group as a whole, (b) the importance attached to group activities (content of group program) and social interaction processes, and (c) the orientation of goals toward therapy, development, or both. Group process and behavior, and intervention concepts referred to the concepts underlying the methods and techniques utilized in group work practice.

Kaiser also pointed out that a number of principles or assumptions already had been formulated and incorporated into the developing body of knowledge underlying group work practice. Thus knowledge about group formation; size of groups; group composition and the degree of homogeneity with respect to age, sex, interests, and cultural background; expressed or implicit purposes of the group; nature of interests for group activity; group structure and controls; quality of interpersonal relations; and *"esprit de corps"* or "group feeling" were identified as factors which constituted group work knowledge. Kaiser noted the need for research directed toward testing knowledge assumptions about the relation between group qualities and goal attainment.

Kaiser (1980) and others (Alissi, 1980; Roberts & Northen, 1976; Toseland & Rivas, 1984) have noted that much knowledge about group processes underlying group work practice has been borrowed from multiple disciplines such as sociology, psychiatry, social psychology, and other social and behavioral sciences. However, Kaiser challenged social group workers to take part in knowledge advancement. The Committee on Practice of the Group Work Section of NASW undertook this task by developing a frame of reference for social group work. The elements of group work described by the Committee were settings, focus, purposes, knowledge, technical skills, and values. The description of these elements was presented in 1984 by Hartford (1980) and represents the attempts, during the early 1960s, to elaborate components of the knowledge base for social work practice with groups.

Practice theory and technical skills. As components of the knowledge base for group work practice, existing practice theory and technical skills have evolved from practice wisdom and clinical experience, tested knowledge,and the integration and application of knowledge from the social and behavioral sciences. Conceptual models of social group work practice, which were developed during the 1960s and 70s, significantly contributed to theory building. Some of the models developed were classified as developmental, functional, organizational, problem solving, psychosocial, reciprocal, remedial or rehabilitative, social goals, socialization, task-centered, crisis-intervention, and behavioral (Alissi, 1980; Roberts & Northen, 1976; Papell and Rothman, 1966).

Theoretical differences among the various models of group work practice were identified early in the development of theory for group work practice. On the basis of an analysis of these differences, Schwartz (1964) classified existing models into three categories: (1) medical, (2) scientific or problem solving, and (3) reciprocal (Northen & Roberts 1976). Papell & Rothman (1966) also classified social group work approaches into three theoretical models: social goals, remedial, and reciprocal. Other classifications of group work practice models have been considered (Home & Darveau-Fournier, 1982). The specification of these models emphasized key concepts and assumptions, the role of the worker, and otherwise described practice principles, especially related to assessment and implementation.

In a review of the then current theories of social work with groups, Roberts and Northen (1976) concluded that there were many areas of agreement about conceptual and empirical knowledge related to the knowledge base of group work practice. Differences between approaches were also noted as suggestive of areas for further theory building and research. Directions for research were identified; however, the greatest need was specified as the need "for research to determine if the theoretical orientations of practitioners make a difference in worker activity, group process, and outcome with different types of clients with different types of presenting problems in different types of agency programs" (p. 393).

Group Work Knowledge and Research

Several surveys of the group work literature undertaken to assess the existing knowledge in social group work have documented the need for research findings to contribute empirical knowledge to the existing knowledge base for social group work practice (Feldman, 1987; Rothman & Fike, 1988; Russell, 1990; Silverman, 1966). A recent survey of the literature regarding social work practice with groups in health care revealed a need for research also on practice with groups in health settings including research on process, planning, intervention skills, and outcome (Northen, 1989).

The paucity of systematic research programs for the evaluation of social work intervention also was noted by Rose, Tallant, Tolman, and Subramanian (1987). Brower and Rose (1990) noted the scarcity of current research about the group as a whole and group processes. They also pointed out the fact that much of the existing research is either over-simplistic or excessively technological. The possible explanation offered for this state of affairs was that research on group work practice was complicated by problems related to conceptualization, design, and analysis with respect to group functioning and group life.

Group research issues. Problems associated with research on group work practice were specified in a recent report by Brower and Rose (1990). Those problems included the expense related to obtaining an adequate sample when control group experimental designs are employed; ethical constraints with respect to withholding services from subjects; difficulty in applying multivariate methods when a large number of uncontrolled variables exist; and measurement and analysis of the effects of individual attributes, individual-group interactions, group conditions and leader attributes and interventions.

Potential evaluation components have been specified by Fike (1980), who urged group intervention evaluators to utilize two or more of five discrete kinds of group evaluation research data: (1) *single subject* (2) *grouped outcome* (3) *group characteristic* (4) *member satisfaction* and (5) *leader characteristics and contributions.* These variables were classified and described to enhance clarity about variables and their potential interrelationship in group evaluation research. Member characteristics influence both group processes and group outcomes (Glisson, 1987; Rose, 1981) therefore, member attribute data can be conceptualized as either independent or dependent variables in group evaluative research (Fike, 1980). Differentiating classes of outcomes, particularly ultimate, instrumental, and intermediate, is relevant to group work research with regard to variables such as member attributes, individual-group interactions, group conditions and leader attributes.

Conceptual and empirical issues related to the use of the individual versus the group as the unit of analysis in small group research has been examined by Glisson (1987). Specifically, the practices of (1) drawing conclusions about groups on the basis of data representing observed relationships among variables characterizing individuals, and (2) aggregating response of individuals to characterize group phenomena may lead to misleading results. Glisson suggests that more theoretical and empirical attention be given to this issue.

Design problems inherent to group work research were addressed by Brower and Garvin (1989). Five commonly used research approaches were identified: experimental methods, individual-within-the-group methods, field outcome studies, case descriptive methods, and SYMLOG and other act-by-act-observational scoring methods. The authors believe that research related to social group work must be multivariate in design and analysis; that variables should be clearly identified as independent, dependent, or intervening, with research consumers' utilization needs taken into account, and that individual outcomes must be examined utilizing an individual-within-the-group-approach. There is also a need to (1) develop programs of research, (2) standardize reporting of results, and (3) develop research and analysis strategies that will handle the complex interactions of group variables (Brower & Rose, 1990).

In spite of the difficulties involved in group work research, empirical knowledge is accumulating. Examples of studies which have attempted to develop design strategies to address many of the prevalent research design problems have been described by Brower and Rose (1990). In addition, researchers are examining the effects of leader characteristics on group behavior (Brower, Garvin, Hobson, Reed, & Reed, 1987) and the effects of group attributes on group outcomes (Rose, 1981). Others are engaging in developmental research (Garvin, 1987; Rose et al., 1987; Rose & Farber, 1990). The use of qualitative and quantitative data in the development of a clinical program also has been described (Rose & Farber, 1990). Current developments in clinical social work research that may be applicable to group work research include meta-analysis (Tallant, 1987), and clinical trials (Cnaan, 1991).

DEVELOPMENT OF EMPIRICAL KNOWLEDGE FOR GROUP WORK PRACTICE

A broad-based concept of empirical practice, which includes a suprastructure and encompasses the three major functions of social work research (Reid, 1987) provides a feasible framework for increasing the empirical base of group work practice. Such a framework would provide safeguards against problems inherent in the knowledge-building process, such as diffusion and narrowness, and lack of effective systems of communication for the systematic development of information (Burns, 1965).

The knowledge base for social work practice consists of a system of at least three types of knowledge: empirical, hypothetical, and assumptive knowledge (Boehm, 1958). Each of these knowledge components is viewed as essential to the knowledge-building process. Further, the knowledge base for group work practice is one important component of the social work knowledge base, which is sufficiently developed to permit the testing of a variety of hypotheses and theories related to (1) various aspects of group process, and (2) the practice of group work, with all its complexities.

Research competence within the profession is developing, in part, due to the impact on the profession of increased personnel at the doctoral level. Other influences include knowledge derived from the research experiences of social work researchers and practitioners, and the movement in social work education toward developing practitioners with research competencies. A scientific orientation toward practice, as well as research expertise are needed to enhance the empirical knowledge base for the social work profession and for group work practice. Also needed are resources to support the research enterprise.

The seed for empirical practice was sown years ago at the Western Reserve Workshop on Social Work Research (White, 1948). The organizers of this workshop acknowledged the contributions to the social work knowledge base that were being made and could be made by other disciplines. However, they recognized the responsibility for knowledge development of educators, practitioners, and students of social work. The participants of the 1947 workshop agreed that research needs should be identified and prioritized; that social workers should develop whatever research methods were required to achieve social work purposes; and that the resources to conduct research needed to be coordinated and expanded. Schools of social work were expected to provide leadership, plan programs of research, and obtain funding.

The rationale for Schools of Social Work to assume leadership and primary responsibility for research was based on (1) their university connections, (2) their responsibility for teaching research and developing plans for training research personnel, and (3) their ability to get funds for systematic research (White, 1948). Proposals for the organization of research in schools included the following:

(a) student research, both master's theses and doctoral dissertations
(b) school research program and research budget
(c) collaborative arrangements between schools of social work and local, state, and national social agencies
(d) setting priorities among certain research endeavors
(e) publication of findings for critical appraisal as a mechanism for advancement of knowledge in social work

Research and Social Work Education

Council on Social Work Education Curriculum Policy requires the integration of research content throughout the curriculum such that students develop an understanding and appreciation of a scientific, analytic approach to knowledge building and practice; and are prepared to evaluate their own practice systematically (CSWE, 1982, 1988). The importance of preparing students who are capable of developing personal systems of empirically based practice has been emphasized (Schuerman, 1977). With regard to curriculum content on social work practice with groups, Anderson (1987) proposed three avenues for research practice integration: (1) use of empirical process in all practice; (2) build instrumentation into group work practice; and (3) use of single system designs for evaluation group work practice.

Rothman and Fike (1987) have urged group work educators to view compliance with CSWE curriculum requirements as an opportunity to enrich research competence in group work and to increase the production of group work research. "Activating practice faculty in research" was considered critical to the education of "group work practitioner/researchers" (p. 98).

Radical structural changes in the research curriculum and some restructuring of institutional patterns and relationships were believed to be necessary to increase research production and to educate "group work practitioner/researchers." Among the changes proposed were (1) faculty development, such that faculty become producers of research; (2) development of alliances between schools and social work practitioners to facilitate research undertakings; and (3) development of research centers to provide a base for practice research.

Development of Research Capability in Social Work

A recent commentary on research development in social work was presented by Austin (1991). Austin identified as a problem, the ambivalence within professional membership organizations about resources to be devoted within the profession to support research development. He noted the fact that "there is no national program within the organized profession . . . for the support and development of research capability throughout the profession" (Austin, 1991, p. 40). He mentioned, also, that it is generally assumed within the practice community that the "university" (including the professional schools and individual faculty members) is responsible for the development of research resources. These comments emphasize the lack of effective leadership within social work practice and education as far as research for the profession is concerned. This lack of leadership impedes the development of research capability in group work practice.

The absence of a systematic pattern of research collaboration between schools and practice settings was identified by Austin (1991), as one problem in developing a distinctive research career track in social work. This problem impacts the availability of research experiences for all students and poses obstacles for social work practitioners and researchers who wish to conduct practice research. The components needed to develop a professional tradition that includes and values research-practitioner career specialists were specified as:

> systematic action by an organized profession and by the network of professional education programs. . .
>
> development of systematic methods for funding . . .
>
> internal changes in both the structure of institutional culture of professional schools and in the organizational culture of the profession. (Austin, 1991, p. 41)

The need for new approaches for collaboration with practitioners was emphasized.

The research prior to 1947 was described as the "emergency hook and ladder" type that could also be characterized as studies that "jes growed" (White, 1948). A more deliberate research approach needs to be adopted by the profession. A better organized agenda would enhance the production of research for group work practice and thus, contribute to the construction of an empirical foundation for social work with groups. Construction of an empirical foundation for group work practice requires a suprastructure to direct the research enterprise, set the research agenda, secure funding, and ensure that empirical knowledge derived from research will be communicated, made public, and disseminated effectively. An empirical foundation for group work practice must also rest on a professional tradition which values the production and utilization of scientific research as essential components of the knowledge-building process.

REFERENCES

Alissi, A. S. (1990). Social group work: Commitments and perspectives. In A. S. Alissi (Ed.), *Perspectives on social group work practice* (pp. 5-35). New York: The Free Press.

Anderson, J. D. (1987). Integrating research and practice in social work with groups. *Social Work with Groups, 9*(3), 111-124.

Ashford, J. B., & LeCroy, C. W. (1991). Problem-solving in social work practice. *Research on Social Work Practice, 1*(3), 306-318.

Austin, D. (1991). Comments on research development in social work. *Social Work Research and Abstracts, 27*(1), 38-41.

Blenkner, M. (1950). Obstacles to evaluative research in social casework. *Social Casework, 31*, 54-60, 97-105.

Bloom, M., & Fischer, J. (1982). *Evaluating practice: Guidelines for the accountable professional.* Englewood Cliffs, NJ: Prentice-Hall.

Boehm, W. W. (1958). The nature of social work. *Social Work, 3*, 10-18.

Briar, S. (1977). Incorporating research into education for clinical practice in social work: Toward a clinical science in social work. In A. Rubin & A. Rosenblatt (Eds.), *Sourcebook on research utilization* (pp. 132-140). New York: Council on Social Work Education.

Briar, S. (1990). Empiricism in clinical practice: Present and future. In L. Videka-Sherman & W. J. Reid (Eds.), *Advances in clinical social work research* (pp. 1-7). Silver Spring, MD: National Association of Social Workers.

Brower, A. M., & Garvin, C. D. (1989). Design issues in social group work research. *Social Work with Groups, 12*(3), 91-102.

Brower, A. M., Garvin, C. D., Hobson, J., Reed, B. G., & Reed, H. (1987). Exploring the effects of leader gender and race on group behavior. In J. Lassner, K. Powell, & E. Finnegan (Eds.), *Social group work: Competence and values in practice* (pp. 129-148). Binghamton, NY: The Haworth Press, Inc.

Brower, A. M., & Rose, S. D. (1990). The group work research dilemma. *Social Work with Groups,* 1-7.

Burns, M. E. (1965). Paths to knowledge: Some prospects and problems. *Journal of Education for Social Work. 1*(1), 13-17.

Cnann, R. A. (1991). Applying clinical trials in social work practice. *Research on Social Work Practice, 1*(2), 139-161.

Council on Social Work Education (1982). Curriculum policy for the master's degree and baccalaureate degree programs in social work education. *Handbook of accreditation standards and procedures.* Washington, DC: Author.

Coyle, G. L. (1930). *Social process in organized groups.* New York: Smith.

Coyle, G. L. (1980). Some basic assumptions about social group work. In A. S. Allissi (Ed.), *Perspectives on social group work practice* (pp. 36-51). New York: The Free Press.

Dean, R. G. (1989). Ways of knowing in clinical practice. *Clinical Social Work Journal, 17*(2), 116-127.

Dean, R. G., & Fenby, B. L. (1989). Exploring epistemologies: Social work action as a reflection of philosophical assumptions. *Journal of Social Work Education, 25,* 46-54.

Deutschberger, P. (1948). *Research in social work.* Unpublished master's thesis, Wayne University.

Fanshel, D. (1980). The future of social work research: Strategies for the coming years. In D. Fanshel (Ed.), *Future of social work research* (pp. 3-18). Washington, DC: National Association of Social Workers.

Feldman, R. A. (1987). Group work knowledge: A two-decade comparison. *Social Work with Groups, 9,* 7-14.

Fike, D. (1980). Evaluating group intervention. *Social Work with Groups, 3,* 41-51.

Fischer, J. (1981). The social work revolution. *Social Work, 26,* 199-207.

Fischer, J. (1984). The Revolution, schmevolution: Is social work changing or not? *Social Work, 29,* 71-74.

French, D. G. (1952). *An approach to measuring results in social work.* New York: Columbia University Press.

Galinsky, M. J., & Schopler, J. H. (1977). Warning: Groups may be dangerous. *Social Work, 22*(2), 89-94.

Garvin, C. (1987). Developmental research for task-centered group work with chronic mental patients. *Social Work with Groups, 9,* 31-42.

Glasser, P. H., & Garvin, C. D. (1976). An organizational model. In R. Roberts & H. Northen (Eds.), *Theories of social work with groups* (74-115). New York: Columbia University Press.

Glisson, C. (1987). The group versus the individual as the unit of analysis in small group research. *Social Work with Groups, 9*(3), 15-30.

Gordon, W. E. (1952). The professional base of social work research. Some essential elements. *Social Work Journal, 33*, 17-22.

Gordon, W. E. (1953). The future of social work research. *Social Work, 3*(4), 99-106.

Gordon, W. E. (1983). Social work: Revolution or evolution? *Social Work, 28*, 181-185.

Greenwood, E. (1957). Social work research: A decade of reappraisal. *Social Service Review, 31*, 311-320.

Hartford, M. E. (1980). Frame of reference for social group work. In A. S. Alissi (Ed.), *Perspectives on social group work practice* (pp. 64-71). New York: The Free Press.

Hartman, A. (1990). Many ways of knowing. *Social Work, 35*, 3-4.

Heineman-Pieper, M. (1988). Comments on "Research paradigms in social work: From stalemate to creative synthesis." *Social Service Review, 56*(2), 246-258.

Home, A., & Darveau-Fournier, L. (1982). A study of social work practice with groups. *Social Work with Groups, 5*, 19-34.

Imre, R. W. (1984). The nature of knowledge in social work. *Social Work, 29*, 41-45.

Ivanoff, A., & Blythe, B. J. (1989). Exploring epistemologies: The debate continues, letter to the editor. *Journal of Social Work Education, 25*(2), 176-197.

Ivanoff, A., Blythe, B. J., & Briar, S. (1987). The empirical clinical practice debate. *Social Casework, 68*, 290-293.

Jayaratne, S., & Levy, R. L. (1979). *Empirical clinical practice.* New York: Columbia University Press.

Kahn, A. J. (1954). The nature of social work knowledge. In C. Kasius (Ed.), *New directions in social work* (pp. 194-214). New York: Harper & Bros.

Kaiser, C. (Ed.). (1930). *The group records of four clubs at the University Settlement Center.* Cleveland: Western Reserve University.

Kaiser, C. A. (1980). The social group work process. In A. S. Alissi (Ed.), *Perspectives on social group work practice* (pp. 52-63). New York: The Free Press.

Karger, H. J. (1983). Science, research, and social work: Who controls the profession? *Social Work, 28*, 200-205.

Karpf, M. J. (1931). *The scientific basis of social work research.* New York: National Association of Social Workers.

Kirk, S. A. (1979). Understanding research utilization in social work. In A. Rubin & A. Rosenblatt (Eds.), *Sourcebook on research utilization* (pp. 3-15). New York: Council on Social Work Education.

Kirk, S. A. (1990). Research utilization: The substance of belief. In L. Videka-Sherman & W. S. Reid (Eds.), *Advances in clinical social work research* (pp. 233-250). Silver Spring, MD: National Association of Social Workers.

Lang, N. C. (1979). A comparative examination of therapeutic uses of groups in social work and in adjacent human service professions: Part II-The literature from 1969-1978. *Social Work with Groups, 2*(2), 197-220.

LeCroy, C. W. (1990). Opening the door to knowledge utilization. In L. Videka-Sherman & W. J. Reid (Eds.), *Advances in Clinical Social Work Research* (p. 262-264). Silver Spring, MD: National Association of Social Workers.

Levinson, H. M. (1973). Use and misuse of groups. *Social Work,* 18(1), 66-73.

Maas, H. S. (1977). Research in social work. In J. B. Twiner (Ed.), *Encyclopedia of social work* (17th ed., pp. 1183-1193). Washington, DC: National Association on Social Workers.

MacDonald, M. E. (1960). Social Work research: A perspective. In N. A. Polansky (Ed.), *Social Work Research* (pp. 1-23). Chicago: The University of Chicago Press.

Newstetter, W. I. (1947). The social intergroup work process: How does it differ from social group work process? In *Community Organization.* New York: Russell Sage Foundation.

Northen, H. (1987). Selection of groups as the preferred modality of practice. In J. Lassner, K. Powell, & E. Finnegan (Eds.), *Social Group Work* (pp. 19-33). Binghamton, NY: The Haworth Press.

Northen, H. (1989). Social work practice with groups in health care. *Social Work with Groups, 12*(4), 7-26.

Northen, H., & Roberts, R. W. (1976). The status of theory. In R. W. Roberts & H. Northen (Eds.), *Theories of social work with groups.* New York: Columbia University Press.

Papell, C. P., Rothman, B. (1966). Social group work models: Possession and heritage. *Journal of Education for Social Work,* 2, 66-77.

Peile, C. (1988). Research paradigms in social work: From stalemate to creative synthesis. *Social Service Review, 62,* 1-19.

Polansky, N. A. (1971). Research in social work. In R. Morris (Ed.), *Encyclopedia of Social Work* (16th ed., pp. 1099-1106). New York: National Association of Social Workers.

Reid, W. J. (1983). Research developments. *1983-84 Supplement to the Encyclopedia of Social Work,* (pp. 128-135). Silver Spring, MD: National Association of Social Workers.

Reid, W. J. (1987). Research in social work. In A. Minahan (Ed.), *Encyclopedia of Social Work,* (18th ed., pp. 474-487). Silver Spring, MD: National Association of Social Workers.

Reid, W. J., & Smith, A. D. (1981). *Research in social work.* New York: Columbia University Press.

Richey, C. A., Blythe, B. J., & Berlin, S. B. (1987). Do social workers evaluate their practice? *Social Work Research & Abstracts, 23,* 14-20.

Richmond, M. E. (1917). *Social diagnosis.* New York: Russell Sage Foundation.

Roberts, R. W., & Northen, H. (Eds.), (1976). *Theories of social work with groups.* New York: Columbia University Press.

Rose, S. D., & Farber, N. (1990). The use of qualitative and quantitative data in the development of a clinical program. In L. Videka-Sherman & W. J. Reid (Eds.), *Advances in clinical social work research* (pp. 174-180). Silver Spring, MD: National Association of Social Workers.

Rose, S. D. (1981). How group attributes relate to outcome in behavior group therapy. *Social Work Research and Abstracts, 17*(3), 25-29.

Rose, S. D., Tallant, S. H., Tolman, R., & Subramanian K. (1987). A multimethod group approach: Program development research. *Social Work with Groups, 9*, 71-88.

Rosen, A., & Mutschler, E. (1982). Social work students' and practitioners' orientation to research. *Journal of Education for Social Work, 18*, 62-68.

Rosenblatt, A. (1968). The practitioner's use and evaluation of research. *Social Work, 13*, 53-59.

Rothman, B., & Fike, D. (1987). To seize the moment: Opportunities in the CSWE standards for group work research. *Social Work with Groups, 10*(4), 91-109.

Russell, M. N. (1990). *Clinical social work: Research and practice*. Newbury Park: Sage Publications.

Schuerman, J. R. (1977). On research and practice teaching in social work. In A. Rubin & A. Rosenblatt (Eds.), *Source-book on research utilization* (143-149). New York: Council on Social Work Education.

Schuerman, J. R. (1987). Passion, analysis and technology: The Social Service Review lecture. *Social Service Review, 61*, 3-18.

Schwartz, W. (1964). Analysis of papers presented on working definitions of group work practice. In M. E. Hartford (Ed.), *Working papers toward a frame of reference for social group work* (p. 60). New York: NASW.

Shilling, R. F. (1990). Making research usable. In L. Videka-Sherman & W. J. Reid (Eds.), *Advances in clinical social work research* (pp. 256-260). Silver Spring, MD: National Association of Social Workers.

Siegel, D. H. (1984). Defining empirically based practice. *Social Work, 29*(4), 325-331.

Silverman, M. (1966). Knowledge in social group work: A review of the literature. *Social Work, 11*(3), 56-62.

Social Work Research Group (1955). *The function and practice of research in social work*. New York: National Association of Social Workers.

Tallant, S. H. (1987). Meta-analysis: Statistical considerations and applications in small group treatment research. *Social Work with Groups, 9*(3), 43-53.

Thyer, B. A. (1991). Exploring epistemologies: The debate continues. Letter to the editor. *Journal of Social Work Education, 25*(2) 174-176.

Thyer, B. A. (Eds.), (1991). *Research on Social Work Practice, 1* (Sage Publications).

Toseland, R. W., & Rivas, R. F. (1984). *An introduction to group work practice*. New York: Macmillan Publishing Co.

Tripodi, T. (1984). Trends in research publication: A study of social work journals from 1956-1980. *Social Work, 29*, 353-359.

White, R. C. (Ed.). (1948). *Research in social work: A report of the workshop on research in social work.* New York: American Association of Social Workers and Cleveland, Ohio: School of Applied Social Sciences, Western Reserve University.

Witkin, S. L. (1991). Empirical clinical practice: A critical analysis. *Social Work, 36*(2), 158-163.

Wood, K. M. (1980). Experiences in teaching the practitioner-researcher model. In R. W. Weinbach & A. Rubin (Eds.), *Teaching social work research* (pp. 13-22). New York: Council on Social Work Education.

Wood, K. M. (1990). Epistemological issues in the development of social work practice knowledge. In L. Videka-Sherman, & W. J. Reid (Eds.), *Advances in clinical social work research* (pp. 373-390). Silver Spring, MD: National Association of Social Workers.

Zimbalist, S. E. (1977). *Historic themes and landmarks in social welfare research.* New York: Harper & Row.

Chapter 6

Group Work for What?
Group Work Linkage of Micro-
and Macro- Social Policy Issues

Bernard J. Wohl

Do we, as social workers, think to ask, to act? The impulse to do so is in our history, but it is a history of long ago and far away. Jane Addams called the impulse "the experimental effort to aid in the solution of the social and industrial problems which are engendered by the modern conditions of life . . . . It is an attempt to relieve. . . the overaccumulation at one end of the society and the destitution at the other."

To be honest, I have to ask myself whether I have found a way to raise the large social issues of equity and justice as the matrix shaping the daily program in my community center. And I have to answer that I have not. The daily crises and decisions command us. We do struggle against the brutalities of homelessness and the disasters of AIDS. We work to treasure children and their possibilities in Head Start, our Day Care Center, and our youth programs. We try to engage our diverse racial and ethnic constituencies in the treasuring of their specific history and heritage and the celebration of skills and knowledge that can come out of the richness of cross-cultural interchange. We house the elderly and the handicapped, counsel hundreds about their options for education, work, and a life of dimension.

At our best, we do exciting social group work with children, teens, and their families. But when we are hit with the broad social policies under which we live as citizens, we find–I find–I am at a loss for tools of change.

The convenient wisdom is that as a nation we are out of funds for domestic social purposes–for health, for housing, for effective education for all our children. The use of tax money for intervention in Central America, the Middle East, and South America is not questioned.

The transformation of our tax structure to favor the haves, the cut in the transfer of funds to the states, the drop-dead prescription for the cities are not questioned.

Projected budget cuts in social services, health, welfare, culture, and education elicit our protests, even our concerted protests. This is clearly an advance beyond internecine struggles over which programs should be cut over others, but we have not yet forged effective weaponry to struggle for different macro social policies.

The last decade of porno politics, of racist images in TV election campaign bites, of the McCarthy-like smearing of the word "liberal," has laid a heavy silence on dissent and dialogue.

Making millions of dollars on shady bank deals by persons close to the wielders of power is seen as routine free enterprise, but compassion for those at the raw edge of poverty is condemned as costly soft-headed "liberalism."

WHERE TO START?

Barbara Kingsolver (1988) in *The Bean Trees,* an adventurous novel set in Kentucky, Arizona, and Oklahoma, captures the sense of despair people feel who witness anguish and cannot find ways to "change anything." In an agony of personal pain about the sexual abuse of her little girl, a woman cries out to a friend:

> "I don't know where to start, Lou Ann . . . . There's just so damn much ugliness. I'm just not up to the job, Lou Ann . . . ."

> "Well, don't feel like the Lone Ranger," she said. "Nobody is."

Are we? No one is up to the job alone. But can people trained in social group work find ways to do what, according to our by-laws, the purposes of our Association enjoin us to do–to "Become a proactive social force in promoting the betterment of society through the use of groups with particular attention to oppressed groups"?

There was a newspaper cartoon recently that sketched all the doors to education, housing, health clinics, drug treatment centers, recreation and cultural halls with bars across them, marked closed. The only door wide open was the door to prisons.

The cartoon did not depict the occupants. No need. They are known. The jailed are predominantly the minority people of oppressed groups.

What are some of the steps to become a "proactive social force"? I must share with you that in the past few months, after I had submitted an abstract for a presentation here, I felt so depressed by the war in the Middle East and its aftermath, the drastic budget cuts in New York City, the robberies of the Bank of Credit and Commerce International (BCCI) added to the robberies of the Savings and Loans, and the shadow of a regressive Supreme Court into the next century, that I felt, with the women of *The Bean Trees,* that I wasn't up to it. How can we fight back against such a massive sea of troubles? The large picture was dominated by power and privilege. Our local energies were fractured by reactive triage and the salvage of budgeting wreckage.

Depression is a solitary illness. The grace, power, and effectiveness of social group work, when we remember our skill, uproots isolation and pushes us back into the social cauldron of struggle.

There is a nasty, national ethos of greed and corruption, a plethora of racism, and the reign of the liar not yet exposed by a smoking gun. But there are also undercurrents of recognition that something is wrong, that our domestic life is being undercut by economic and civil loss.

We need to reclaim our knowledge that in social groups people can give each other their possibilities of renewal and change in a common fight for economic and social justice.

Recapturing Our Resources: Reclaiming Our Taxes

The struggle against massive budget cuts in New York this past year had some new dimensions. Groups did not battle against one another–the litany of suffering was appalling everywhere, and a common strategy was sought. It was clear that the hardest blows would fall on minority communities. Despite the usual difficulties, the Community Service Society of New York, the New York State Black and Puerto Rican Legislative Caucus, the State Communities Aid Association, the Association of Puerto Rican Executive Directors, the Black Agency Executives, the Federation of Protestant Welfare Agencies, the African-American Institute, the Federation of Jewish Philanthropies, United Neighborhood Houses of New York (whose members consist of the settlements and community centers of the city), many unions, and countless social, cultural, educational and health agencies, proposed alternatives, marched, protested, and petitioned together for better choices for a different city and state tax structure, and impact.

But glaringly absent was a concerted, macro attempt to challenge the federal restructuring under Reagan of the national system of taxation. The Reagan re-do of the structure of taxation enhanced the prosperity of the rich. Responsibilities previously shouldered by the federal government were shifted to the states and cities, but the percentage of taxes returned to the states was decimated.

Protesters felt that efforts to reverse the tax policy of the federal government would be useless in today's climate, and in any case would not help this year. But next year is reputed to be worse. No fundamental relief is possible unless the federal tax structure is altered. The bulk of taxes goes to Washington. The upcoming tax burdens to sew up the gashes of the S and L heist have yet to be endured. The states and cities cannot shoulder these massive burdens alone. Only a just tax structure on a federal level can recapture our resources for productive recovery.

Our Social Action Committee can be instrumental in raising a different perspective than exists today, a national perspective of fair burdens for a democratic polity to replace favors for the powerful. Mayors and governors need to feel the push of their constituencies for a national restructuring of taxation. Mayors and governors cannot do more with less as the trickle down dries up. Many have already appealed to Washington's deaf ear, but Washington has been insulated from the clamor below. The clamor needs macro orchestration.

The members of the Association for the Advancement of Social Work with Groups have the skills of collaboration and coalition with other organizations and movements. The pressures to deal with the local trauma on our own doorstep are enormous and cannot be postponed, but the way in which we deal with them can be enlarged to define the origins of imbalance and deficit and the path to change.

The Community Service Society of New York's report, *Poor Choices: The Impact of the Governor's Proposed Budget on New York City, Fiscal Year 1991-92,* charged that much of New York State's deficit is structural in nature, an outcome of a dysfunctional state tax system, but it did not sharply relate that deficit to the basic dysfunction of the national tax system. That is the macro task of social policy–to relate immediate protests and organizational mobilization to a basic strategy for change at the source of the problem.

Civil Rights and Racism

The last decade has also witnessed the erosion of civil rights won over twenty years of street protest, organized social struggle, and legal challenge in the courts. The federal government has packed the Supreme Court with judges ready to reverse whatever gains were made by minority groups in employment and education and by women in the control of their reproductive lives.

Civil rights are under siege not only in the courts, but in the workplace, in employment and in education. The Willie Horton distortion was used in the political arena for racist advantage. The "quota" distortion was used to reverse legal precedents in employment and education.

This climate has darkened every aspect of public life. Multiculturalism is being pilloried in the media and in discussion about educational goals and direction as a play against national unity. Under attack are initiatives to discover through interchange across multiple diversities, the strengths of personal and group identity and the human treasure to be mined out of the richness of our cultural and historical differences.

Buried in the smears against multiculturalism is a policy of racist denigration of "inferiors" by the "superior" cohort of the culture.

In an unpublished letter to the Editor of *The New York Times*, Beth Singer, Chairperson of the Philosophy Department at Brooklyn College, recalled the address of the American philosopher John Dewey to the National Education Association in 1916.

He said to the assembled teachers, "I wish our teaching of American history in the schools would take more account of the great waves of migration by which our land for over three centuries has been continuously built up, and make every pupil conscious of the rich breadth of our national make-up. When every pupil recognizes all the factors which have gone into our being, he will continue to prize and reverence that coming from his own past, but he will think of it as honored in being simply one factor in forming a whole nobler and finer than itself." He warned, "unless our education is nationalized in a way which recognizes that the peculiarity of our nationalism is its internationalism, we shall breed enmity and division in our frantic efforts to secure unity."

That was 75 years ago. The greater recent "waves of migration," spun out by the convulsions of wars, of exile and hunger and fear, have brought new tides of immigrants from Africa and Asia and Central and South America of myriad ethnic, racial, and cultural backgrounds. Dewey's warning is more cogent now that it was three-quarters of a century ago.

The New York Times (front page 3/11/91) described the speed at which the country's racial and ethnic mix was altered in the 1980s as "breathtaking."

> "The racial and ethnic complexion of the American population changed more dramatically in the past decade than at any time in the twentieth century, with nearly one in every four Americans claiming African, Asian, Hispanic or American Indian ancestry. The 1980 census found that one in five Americans had a minority background."

It is a monumental failure of democratic imagination to fear the fabric and design of difference. It is disgraceful that the discussion of multiculturalism today is conducted in a haggler's market of shopworn racism and anti-Semitism.

Social work has a command of a different language to pierce this discussion. Our historic leaders, not many in number but of powerful voice, were, by living their philosophy, related to the poor and the oppressed, to immigrant groups, to those excluded from privilege.

The clients of social service agencies, of settlement houses and community centers, are still the poor and the oppressed, and the racial, ethnic, and immigrant minorities. When we exercise our skill in knowledge in social group work they become advocates of their rights, and the rights of others in common.

There is a history and tradition in social work of weaving service to meet immediate human needs into a framework of working for social change. The constituencies are present–women who will fight against the reversals of their rights and capacities; African Americans, Latinos, legal and illegal immigrants, who reject racism, bigotry, and discrimination; students who are outraged at the rise of racism and anti-Semitism on their college campuses.

The Social Action Committee of our Association in its draft statement signals the transformative values which can generate the strength needed to change macro policies. They are:

- A belief that people acting together can be powerful.
- An emphasis on the competence and capability of people, whether whole or hurt, to give each other their enlarging possibilities.
- An understanding, in attacking complex issues, that oppression, public policy, the environment, and the economy are often stronger forces than personal factors.
- A commitment to discover through interchange across multiple diversities, the strengths of personal and group identity and the human treasure to be mined out of our cultural and historical differences.

Housing

A Program Paper of the Ford Foundation, *Affordable Housing: The Years Ahead,* 1989, concluded: "Housing conditions for the poor have worsened dramatically in the past several years and promise to deteriorate further in the near future. The loss of real income combined with a drastic reduction in federal subsidies pose formidable obstacles for low-income families seeking decent and affordable housing."

It is not only the poor who are at risk of homelessness. *The New York Times* reports (front page, 9/26/90): "Doubling-up, once mainly the plight of the poorest of New York's poor, has now become an affliction of the working class. Inexpensive housing has become so hard to find that the number of families forced to live doubled and tripled-up has increased dramatically . . . ."

The acute suffering of the homeless and the doubled-and tripled-up families forces us to deal with emergencies and extended ordeals on such an impacted and daily basis, that it is hard to pull together the energies and the vision to even articulate the necessary macro policy change–to force the federal government to look to the welfare of the people and to once again resume its responsiblity to provide affordable housing as a common human need.

This is not the only responsibility to be reforged–the city and state also have tasks here, but the crisis in housing cannot be handled without the resources of the federal government.

The group workers in settlement houses and community centers, and their associates in social service, housing, and community-based agencies, can orchestrate the movement from micro to macro, if they jointly develop that vision.

The macro policy issues are as urgent in education, health, employment, war and peace, and the environment as they are in housing, taxation, civil rights, and racism.

How do we move to a vision of social action that relates the tasks of change to the people we work with daily?

Micro Life and the Macro Vision

The expression of that vision is generated by our skill in relating the problems and emergencies of daily life with an understanding of the ways in which those individual blows are intertwined.

Those struggles take place in our social groups. We have great strengths as service providers. People turn to us with their bitter needs or we turn to them with our outreach programs. We find each other. Our work starts with their clients needs for practical assistance and support. The strength of our social groups is that its process can transform clients into participants, participants who become advocates for themselves and for others, who can reshape their own lives and the lives of their communities.

It can happen through the magic of social involvement. People who hurt find the services they need through our efforts, but they can find more. In social groups, they can find their own capacities, limited or large. Through the relationships with staff and with members, people find the new possibilities they give each other.

The process is not smooth. It is attacked daily by the gritty conditions of life and the assaults of the media which focus almost exclusively on crack, crime and chaos in the culture of poverty.

But the connections happen–not always, perhaps not even often, but when they happen, they strengthen confidence and the knowledge of how to design new strategies of connection and social action.

Let me take one example from two of our parent groups, involved with us over program and issues affecting their children, during the height of the protest actions against budget cuts in March of 1991.

Staff had called the parents to an emergency evening meeting to organize for the protest rally in Albany, our state capitol. A projected 54% cut in youth services threatened the programs the parents depend on for their children after school. It was the time of the Iraq war.

I am reporting from a staff record:

It was not just the loss of after school programs that agitated the parents. One of the fathers said: "The Gulf War had more than our share of young people in the military. Our kids' choices were the army or the streets–not jobs or other chances. And that's what is happening again, for our younger ones. Cut out of the budget is everything good, good education and jobs–what's left is the army for those who aren't killed on the streets."

A mother said bitterly: "The old people are sick; the teens are done for already, and now it's the young ones." Another young mother said: "It isn't just Albany on Tuesday. This is our war, and Tuesday is one fight in that war." One of the working parents said she could get off on Tuesday and go to Albany, but she had no one to get her little girl to school if she had to be on the bus to Albany at 6:30 a.m. A mother across the hall called out: "Don't worry, I'll get your girl to school and pick her up after school. Go to Albany."

Other parents who worked could not go. They wanted to know: what else can we do? There were sheets with phone numbers and addresses for calls and letters . . . . parents signed up . . . .

One of the fathers said: "Why are the papers and the TV so quiet on the war against us?"

Another father said: "I'm glad of the people here tonight. This is the best meeting I've seen. I don't know why a dog story makes the whole press but there's nothing about the danger to our kids. We need to do something. This is our war."

Another father said he could not go to Albany but he could visit state senators or assembly members here in the city if others went with him. A staff member asked for parents to work on the budget crisis after Albany and hands went up.

After the meeting a mother went up to the woman who said "our teens are done for" and said to her, "don't give up on our teens yet either. They're hurting, but they're not gone."

And from a staff record on the protest rally:

> On Tuesday the bus took off from in front of the center. On board was a cross section of programs, parents from the Friday night rally, members and staff from our outreach program to the homeless, tenants from the building we rehabilitated for 136 formerly homeless men and women; seniors in their seventies and eighties, participants and staff from our educational counseling program, community organizers from our West Side SRO Law Project and the youth program.

> In Albany they marched with thousands of others . . . .

> At departure time, one of the seniors had not returned to the bus. Two young men streaked from the bus to look for him in the departing floods of demonstrators. Miraculously, they found him in the crowds and brought him back, to travel home together . . . .

Group work, when seen as a laboratory, can experiment and evolve identity and interconnection, the experience of confidence in self, and trust in others while working together for common purpose.

It happens in small groups when social group workers engage participants in the challenges of change, personal and social, for goals they choose and means they design. The steam and satisfaction experienced in micro group engagement can play locomotive to the macro when group workers stoke a vision of equity and justice to counter "what is" as the way of the immutable world of the privileged.

It requires workers of a special stripe to connect the immediate to an unfolding vision which is continually battered by the opposite reality.

It requires stamina to sustain the differences of alliances and coalitions.

Members of this Association have drafted goals for a Social Action Committee that envision macro change.

The goals are to promote:

1. Direct action by the membership of A.A.S.W.G. to marshal the knowledge, methods and skills of social group work to challenge inequity, injustice, and oppression by reason of race, gender, sexual orientation, age, class, religion, or disability.
2. Support of and collaboration with other social work organizations and social movements organizing for universal health care, affordable housing to prevent homelessness, the nurture and protection of children, the rights of the elderly, full employment, civil rights, the defense of the environment and the struggle to defeat discrimination and oppression.
3. The gathering and dissemination of information and the stimulation of dialogue and interchange on the practice and skill of social action groupwork.
4. A renewal of the historic social groupwork commitment to national and international cooperation for peace and the healing of the ravages of famine, dislocation, and grief left by war and oppression.

If anyone is "up to the job" that the women of *The Bean Trees* despaired of alone, it is group workers who are not alone, who are related to each other, and to our constituent groups, micro through macro.

The relationship of micro is not a new issue–it precedes the origins of social work; it is part of the history of the human struggle to relate to the dynamism between the personal and the social.

Social work practitioners and thinkers have debated the issue in the context of every historic period. In 1969 William Schwartz writing in the social Welfare Forum on "Private Troubles and Public Issues: One Social Work Job or Two?" asked: "How can we merge the twin images of individual and social need into one? In a complex and disordered world, there are forces constantly working to pull them apart. . . ."

He quotes C. Wright Mills: "It is the task of the liberal institution . . . . continually to translate troubles into issues and issues into the terms of their human meaning for the individual."

It is surely the task of the school of social work to address this issue in the specific terms of our own time, of the "complex and disordered world" we face. It is also the task of each of us in our own schools or agencies and in the concourse human meaning for the individual."

It is surely the task of the schools of social work to address this issue in the specific terms of our own time, of the "complex and disordered world" we face. It is also the task of each of us in our own schools or agencies and in the concourse of our Association for the Advancement of Social Work with Groups.

REFERENCE

Kingsolver, Barbara (1988). *The Bean Trees*. New York: Harper & Row.

Chapter 7

Developing Professional Identity Through Social Group Work: A Social Development Systems (SDS) Model for Education

Nazneen S. Mayadas
Doreen Elliott

SUMMARY. Social group work came into existence as a response to the need for social reform. It developed alongside social work, and when the profession's pendulum swung from a social change perspective to a therapeutic/medical model, social group work sought its identity in intragroup, psychotherapeutic orientations. This paper suggests that group work, while retaining its therapeutic position, can reinstate the "social" into its repertoire, and regain its lost heritage. In order to move from a unidimensional, unicausal approach to a multioption approach, a new theoretical base is proposed. This chapter offers a model for explaining, analyzing, and intervening in social situations based on the interaction of two theories: general systems and social development. General systems theory contributes to explaining and analyzing. Social development theory offers a value base and intervention strategies for change at varying levels of practice. Interactively, these two theories provide multiple options for description, interpretation, assessment analyses, and intervention.

The contribution of this chapter is (1) in integrating the seemingly varied and disparate tasks of the social group worker within a unified theory, (2) in validating the profession's identity to incorporate both the micro and macro perspectives and strategies for social change, and (3) it extends the ability of social group work, from therapy to social action, to address the needs of the poor and the oppressed.

CONTEXTUAL BASIS FOR AN SDS MODEL OF SOCIAL GROUP WORK

Social work has a diffuse professional identity, in that it is an umbrella term for a range of tasks, including clinical practice, therapy, counseling, community organization and planning, social action, and administration of social service delivery systems. Yet, despite this impressive range of tasks to which it lays claim, social work has emerged as a profession which is trapped within a premise of individualism (Seidman, 1983, p. 313). Despite its early origins in the Charity Organization Society (COS) and Settlement Movements, which were formed out of the need to address the results of poverty, the short history of the profession has led it increasingly to espouse the medical model (Mayadas and Glasser, 1986). It is characterized by the assumption of pathology within the individual, and the expertise of the professional who diagnoses, treats, and cures the identified problem. The medical model is implicit in such apparently differing theoretical approaches as Freudian influenced psychodynamics and Behavioral Interventions.

The early origins of the profession of social work in the Charity Organization Society and the Settlement Movement symbolizes a present-day ideological dichotomy in the values and goals of the profession. Casework with its origins in the COS has today become Therapy and Case Management. The Settlement Movement inspired the group work and community organization approach and reflected to a certain extent a social reform agenda.

This dichotomy is expressed variously as the distinction between micro and macro practice; or the differing approaches of social action and therapy; and sometimes it is expressed as the medical or curative model in contrast to prevention and empowerment. In whatever way these distinctions are conceptualized the fact remains that they have become separate and often conflicting approaches to the profession. The inability to reconcile these different elements theoretically has given social work an ambiguous image. Specht (1990) warns that social work has been taken over by psychotherapy and argues that social work should aim to create healthy people through healthy communities. Wakefield (1988a; 1988b) argues that social work has failed to express clearly its "organizing value" and proposes a model with distributive justice as an organizing value. Reeser and Leighninger (1990) and Saleeby (1990) express similar concerns about the loss of social justice goals in social work. Meyer (1990) argues that we must repair "our fractured profession" and regain the tradition of social reform. Leonard's (1975) early warning that social work theory should not merely be descriptive, but should be prescriptive is still relevant today. Billups (1984, p. 179) suggests:

> Without a strong commitment to adopting a distinctive social work practice frame of reference . . . social work is likely to continue developing an uncoordinated and quite possibly unmanageable proliferation of special practices.

These concerns are backed by empirical data. Swartz and Dattalo (1990) reported that despite expressing interest in macro concentrations in social work training, students overwhelmingly chose micro concentrations. CSWE (1991) data for 1990 show that straight macro options (i.e., community organization and planning, administration and management, or a combination of these) accounted for only 7.3% of social work students in training. On the other hand, direct practice alone accounted for 54.5% and a combination of micro and macro concentrations along with "generic" accounted for a further 19.2%. These training figures reflect the therapeutic trend in social work practice. Increasingly private practice is the preferred mode of service delivery for social work practitioners and social work students aspire to the same goal (Rubin and Johnson, 1984). Garvin (1984) examines the impact of these issues on social group work.

In the 1960s and the 1970s the debate over "radical" social work was alive. However, the move to conservatism in politics, economics, personal values, and religion (in many countries) during the late 1970s and 1980s resulted in a move away from social action and social justice as goals for social work. Instead, the profession looked to empiricism and quantitative methods in research and the medical curative model of therapy as means to improve the credibility and status of the profession.

In essence, social work is predominantly delivered through a residual model of service delivery, there exists a large degree of privatization, and the logical positivist research model is prevalent alongside a medical model of intervention designed to address individual pathology.

Social group work, since the early days of the Settlement Movement, has had a long and symbiotic relationship with the social work profession. Prior to the 1930s the term "group work" was not in frequent use; the terms "clubs, classes, and committees" being the more common terms (Wilson, 1976, p. 17). The first beginnings of an underpinning theory for social group work, were put forward in 1935 by Coyle and Newstetter. The theoretical concepts were then primarily sociological, argues Wilson (1976). Group work is practiced in the professions of education and recreation with whom it was at first closely associated, but Wilson argues the distinguishing feature of social group work is that it is governed by the basic philosophy, values, and methods of the social work profession (1976, p. 38). Indeed, just as the wider profession has been influenced by the medical/therapeutic model, so social group work has become increasingly therapeutically oriented.

The range of social group work models currently used is described in the literature in various taxonomies, classifications, and continua. Some authors describe differing theoretical models: e.g., Behavioral therapy, Psychoanalytic therapy, Existential-Experiential, Psychodrama, Gestalt, Transactional Analysis, Reality therapy, Rational-Emotive therapy (Shaffer and Galinsky, 1974; Corey and Corey, 1990). Other authors focus on the function of groups, for example Hartford (1976, pp. 54-55) classifies groups according to five foci thus: (1) primarily focused on some effect on individual participants; (2) primarily focused on some effect on the relationships between and among participants or on their relationships with others outside of the groups; (3) primarily focused on problem solving or task achievement; (4) primarily focused on affecting the context of the group; (5) primarily focused on affecting an institution outside of the group or the wider group. Lieberman (1975) distinguishes a continuum of groups from psychotherapy dealing with sickness and pathology to personal growth groups aimed at the development of healthy people. Other authors categorize groups by identifying conceptual models related to the goals, functioning, and theoretical orientation of the group. Papell and Rothman (1966) identified the remedial, reciprocal, and social goals models; the Organizational model was particularly associated with the Michigan School (Glasser and Garvin, 1976). The Development Model built by Coyle, Schwartz, and others, has been summarized and developed by Tropp (1976). Maier (1981) offers three typologies and challenges group workers to create their own. Middleman and Wood (1990b) give a good summary of the recent development of group work models. They propose three formulations: Social Group Work, Group Therapy, and Social Work with Groups.

It is clear that the majority of these models focus on individual change through small groups, that the area of change is intrapersonal and interpersonal and that much of what goes on in the name of social group work is considered "treatment" or "therapy" and is aimed to "cure." Middleman and Wood (1990a) point out that despite group methods being widely used by social workers, the teaching of social group work remains obscured by the emphasis placed on one-to-one orientations in "group-oblivious" work. It may be argued that much of group psychotherapy is in fact individual therapy in a group setting. Two studies reviewing a 40-year span of the group work literature (Feldman, 1986; Silverman, 1966) state that to date, social group work has not put forward a unified framework to encompass its disparate functions, and they send out a plea for systematic attention to theory building.

This chapter argues a need for a reframing of the paradigm informing both social work as a profession and social group work as a part of that, to validate and enhance the social change functions (Frankel and Sundel, 1978; Cnaan and Adar, 1987; Breton, 1989). The theoretical basis influencing a profession's activities can have a very significant impact on both the professional identity and prestige of the profession. Witness the growth in influence and prestige of the medical profession following the adoption of the germ theory of disease from the 1870s onward, leading to the establishment of a scientific base for the profession and the development of surgery (Conrad and Schneider, 1985). The power of a paradigm shift is eloquently expressed by Maier (1981, p. 35):

> After all, Kuhn, in his powerful analysis, *The Structure of Scientific Revolution* (1972), teaches us that model or paradigm changes are at the root of scientific revolutions and account for the major advances in the sciences.

It is proposed here that a combination of social development and general system theory supplies a unifying conceptual basis for the education and practice of social group work which is consistent with its historical origins and the broad brief derived from current practice. Although a number of authors have begun to apply social development theory to generic social work practice generally, no attempts have come to light specifically in relation to social group work.

COMPONENTS OF SDS MODEL

Values of Social Development

Social development values represent an ideology close to that of the values of social work, except that the values are less individually focused. Spergel (1977) argues that social development values are consistent with social work values in respect to ideology, worker qualification, use of relationship, influence, scientific method, resource complexity, and constraint. At a general level there is consistency in both approaches in their common focus on human rights and a liberal value perspective. In terms of operationalization, however, it might be argued that social work is essentially individually oriented and politically conservative, while social development is globally and radically oriented. Falk (1984) contends that this need not be so, and that micropractice can be consistent with a social development orientation, since there is a compatible commonality in the value base. Fulfillment of basic human needs, human dignity, equality of means, participatory democracy, and peace, were the values ranked highest in a Delphi-method survey of Social Development values (Falk, 1981). Rose (1990) demonstrates the role of advocacy and empowerment in clinical practice. Omer (1979) stresses the interdisciplinary nature of social development, in that it is an intersectorial, interregional, integrated approach which emphasizes connectedness. In this regard it focuses on the multicausal nature of social issues, avoids simplistic unicausal explanations, and offers multilevel intervention possibilities.

In summary, key elements of social development are to achieve social justice through institutional change, empowerment, conscientization, democratic values, cooperation, regeneration of society, redefining social problems, mutuality of effort across systems and disciplines, and the promotion of human dignity and worth.

Operationalizing Social Development

Two very different concepts are inherent within common usage of the term social development: it represents the socialization of the individual and human growth and behavior classes have traditionally prepared social workers with this individualistic interpretation (Cummings, 1983; Billups, 1990). This may be termed the micro interpretation. The macro interpretation on the other hand, has focused on economic and social change in developing countries: e.g., institution building, empowerment, conscientization, and has been until recently, the practice area of social, economic, and political planners. More recently the literature has begun to address a holistic concept of social development (Paiva, 1977; Omer, 1979; Gil, 1981; Jones and Pandey, 1981; Falk, 1981, 1984; Cummings, 1983; Meinert, Kohn, and Strickler, 1984; Khinduka, 1987; Meinert and Kohn, 1987). While there has been some discussion about the link between social development and social work, the literature remains as yet, at a general level (Spergel, 1977; Hollister, 1977; Midgley, 1984a, 1984b; Sanders, 1987; Billups, 1990). An example of this is the basic process model for social development involving the social work processes of reconnaissance, engagement, assessment, planning, implementation, evaluation, and disengagement presented by Meinert and Kohn (1987).

General System Theory

The general systems approach has been proposed as a generic theoretical base for social work (e.g., Hearn, 1969; Gordon, 1969;

Buckley, 1967; Shulman, 1969; Leighninger, 1977). The focus on the relationship of wholes, parts, and interconnectedness at different system levels, suprasystems, systems, and subsystems, (Bertalanffy, 1950) lends it not only to understanding and analyzing various dimensions of human and social phenomena, from intrapsychic to interorganizational, but also to examining the interconnectedness and impact of parts on various interacting systems, i.e., change in any part of a system is likely to produce corresponding changes in other interrelated systemic parts. Despite this facility of the systems approach, it has failed to fully satisfy the needs of the profession for a wide-ranging holistic theory. It became identified with a conservative adjustment rather than a radical change-oriented approach. While it explains malfunction it does not give the tools for intervention and change. Thus it lacks dynamism and needs to be combined with an action-based model to satisfy both the theoretical and practical base of social work. The concepts of Social Development complement General Systems Theory, in that they provide dynamic strategies for change and skills for intervention across the intrapsychic-interorganizational continuum.

PRESENTATION OF SDS MODEL

Social Development Systems (SDS) Model

The model presented here incorporates a social development theory value base and goals, with general systems theory. Social work itself is multidimensional and has a wide range of goals, and social group work reflects these characteristics of the professional base from which it operates. Thus the use of general system theory interactively with social development, acts as an aid to the identification and analysis of problems. To thus influence the nature and level of intervention is to avoid the pitfalls of individual pathology represented in the traditional medical model.

Figure 8.1 gives a summary of the overall model of how Social Development and General System Theory may be applied to social work, by reviewing its application to the value base, the theoretical context, aspects of operationalizing the concept (i.e., goals, process

FIGURE 8.1. Social Development and General Systems: Toward a Theoretical Model of Social Work

VALUE BASE	SOCIAL DEVELOPMENT	Applicable at individual, family, organization, locality, region, state, national, and international levels.
CONTEXT	SYSTEM THEORY	System Analysis—in line with inter-disciplinary multilevel intervention.
THEORETICAL APPROACH TO METHOD SELECTION	ECLECTIC	Drawing on various approaches as appropriate for the situation: e.g., behavioral, psychodynamic, organizational, humanistic, gestalt, T.A., RET, etc., as consistent with the Social Development Value Base & Systems Analysis of Needs.
OPERATIONALIZATION	GOALS. PROCESS AND SKILLS.	Development through: Goals: Therapy, Organizational Change, Co-unity Development, Social Education (conscientization), and Social Action (empowerment). Process: Assessment, Analysis, Goal Setting, Implementation, Withdrawal, Evaluation. Skills: 3 skill clusters: Analysis, Communication, Action.
QUALITY CONTROL	HEURISTIC PARADIGM OF RESEARCH METHODS	Involving quantitative and qualitative methods. Measurement of individual behavior to social indicators.
EDUCATION AND TRAINING	INTERDISCIPLINARY. EMPHASIS ON TRANSFER OF LEARNING. GENERALIST THROUGH SPECIALIST	Broad knowledge base from Economics, Politics, Sociology, Anthropology, Psychology, Philosophy, Human Geography and Biology, Clinical Practice, Organizational Theory.

and skills), quality control, and education and training. This chapter illustrates operationalizing this model through social group work.

APPLICATION OF SDS MODEL TO GROUP WORK

Goals for Social Group Work

The Social Development Systems Model (SDS) throws a different light on goals of operationalization. Goals are seen as the most important criteria by which groups are identified. The goal of individual change through the group process is an important tradition and function of current practice in social group work and therapy remains a valid goal in this new model. However, the application of the SDS model to therapy may result in the emergence of additional forms of intervention for some clients, as well as a redefinition of the problem. For example, a group of women with eating disorders may be perceived as deviant, sick, or psychologically disturbed in the traditional approach. SDS requires workers to look beyond the intrapsychic and interpersonal system levels to recognize the influence of gender-role expectations, media and popular images of the female body-type, and the consequences of what Saleeby (1990, p. 38) argues may be a distorted and abused identity. Many women's groups would benefit from this broader systems analysis informing the therapeutic intervention: abused women's groups, the problems of women and depression; women who abuse or neglect their children, drug abusers, and homeless women take on a new perspective. There is less likelihood of blaming the victim and new goals of conscientization and empowerment may be joined to the therapeutic effort, while still recognizing that therapy may in some cases be the best immediate and short-term goal. The model not only recognizes the importance of therapy, since social development may be applied at an individual level, but it seeks to expand awareness in assessing problems and to broaden the range of therapeutic strategies.

Therapeutic groups for alcoholics, drug abusers, and juvenile delinquents may be perceived in the same way. Personal responsibility for the deviance, sickness, or problem is not erased, but it is seen in a much broader context.

Other groups may be defined as focusing primarily on organization change, or community development. Currently, most of the social group work literature focuses on intragroup functioning, roles, process, and skills (Middleman & Wood, 1990a). Intergroup functions and skills are not as fully developed. The social development value base and the systems approach of SDS require the worker to look beyond the boundaries of the group.

Figure 8.2 shows two columns. The column headed Intra-Group represents the traditional social group work approaches which focus on intrapersonal and interpersonal processes. Another column is necessary to incorporate the broader mandate which social work claims for the profession. Here in the Inter-Group column, the focus of intervention is on relation to group/environment at different levels–these may be group/group, or group/system interactions. Although the focus may be inter-group, nevertheless the group worker must build on the foundation of intra-group skills in order for the inter-group process to be successful. Thus the columns represented in Figure 8.2 are not mutually exclusive but are interdependent.

An example of how this inter-group perspective might be operationalized follows thus: A Department of Health and Human Services child protective services unit becomes aware that a particular large apartment complex located in a high-rise building in a city is producing a number of child at risk/abuse referrals. The traditional medical model response is to intervene individually in these cases. If groups are held, they might be therapeutic groups for abusing parents. This has some validity since some research studies indicate that abusing parents have often been abused themselves in childhood (Costin, Bell, & Downs, 1991, pp. 342-343). The SDS model, however, would then proceed to further intervention. Research also suggests that abusing parents are often socially isolated, suffer from stress due to illness, poverty, unemployment and may have few child care facilities (Costin, Bell, & Downs, 1991, pp. 327-328). To intervene only at a therapeutic level is to address just part of the multicausal nature of the problem, and to redefine it in a unicausal way. Opportunity for support groups or educational groups focusing on child-rearing or social skills might all have relevance in extending the therapeutic intervention. However, the inter-group dimension might be brought into effect by the creation of a self-help

FIGURE 8.2. Comparison of Traditional and SDS Models of Groups

TRADITIONAL	SOCIAL DEVELOPMENT SYSTEMS (SDS)
	Traditional plus: –
INTRA-GROUP	INTER-GROUP
Focus	**Focus**
Intrapersonal	Group/Environment via: –
Interpersonal	(1) Group/Group(s) Intrasystem
	(2) Group/Group(s) Intersystem
Theory	**Theory**
Humanistic	Social Development
Behavioral	General Systems
Psychodynamic	
RET	
T.A.	
Skill Groups	**Skill Clusters**
e.g., Interpersonal skills	(1) Analysis
Continuous group skills	Systems Analysis
Skills for building groups	Assessment
Skills for facilitating groups	Evaluation of functioning
Skills for activity-focused groups	process & outcome
Skills for dealing with barriers	(2) Communication
Skills for coping with conflict	Mediation
[Middleman & Wood, 1990(a)]	Negotiating
	Bargaining
	Conscientization
	(3) Action
	Advocacy
	Empowerment
	Adaptation
	Change
	Solidarity
Knowledge	**Knowledge**
Group Dynamics:	– Broader range of knowledge from
Structure,	Individual Development/Socialization
Process,	to Economics, Politics, and Social Change.
Evaluation.	

group which might persuade the apartment complex owners to free one apartment for community purposes where a crèche could be established for child care. This would release young mothers trapped in apartments high up in a building with no safe yard in which to allow children to play, to get respite from constant child care demands, and at the same time addressing issues of social isolation. If market forces conspire to operate against the group, then they may try further action to change city or community policies to legislate that every apartment complex be required to provide such community facilities. In the process, the actions of empowerment, adaptation, and advocacy have been operationalized.

Other goals indicated in Figure 8.1 are social education–such as social skills, which when a political factor is involved, may become conscientization, and social reform or empowerment. It is recognized that empowerment needs to be seen as more than individual empowerment. All of these goals may be present at any one time in a group, but the differentiation between groups will be attributed to having one of these as a primary goal, while other goals remain secondary and tertiary. All goals are recognized, but the group is acknowledged on the premise of its primary goal. This stresses the key feature of the SDS Model, that a group can alter its nature and function contingent on how goals are perceived and articulated.

Process

The group process within the SDS theoretical model may be identified as a general social work process illustrated in Figure 8.1 which includes assessment, goal setting, implementation, withdrawal, and evaluation. The process may apply to the whole range of group activity from therapy to social action. However, when placed alongside the social development value base and the systems analysis of need, then the range of assessment for example, is appropriately broadened to preclude a unicausal and pathological view of the situation. Instead, a multicausal understanding may be achieved through the assessment process which views the client within a broad systems context.

The illustration used earlier of the DHS child abuse referral example may be used to highlight this aspect of the SDS Model. If therapy is the primary goal of the group, then the traditional model might emphasize achieving insight into the psychodynamics or stress management and anger control (Galinsky et al., 1978; Fatout, 1987). The SDS model would additionally include insight into sociocultural factors such as gender role expectations in child rearing, and the role of economic deprivation and stress. If intervention moves into the inter-group dimension, then the process may focus on systemic change through coalition formation (Gentry, 1987) or on empowerment in the broad sense, which includes environmental change. In cases such as these, Bakalinsky (1984) suggests that the group will be less process oriented and more task focused.

Skills

Figure 8.1 shows three clusters of skills associated with the SDS model: skills associated with analysis, communication, and action. Figure 8.2 sets out these skills in more detail. The cluster entitled analysis includes processing of data for assessment, monitoring, and evaluation. The communication cluster includes all the traditional, interpersonal skills (Mayadas & Duehn, 1986; Glassman & Kates, 1986) and the specific group skills identified by Middleman and Wood (1990a) but in addition, adds skills such as mediation, bargaining, and negotiating skills. Finally, the action cluster identifies advocacy, empowerment, solidarity, adaptation, and change as important skills for practice from this perspective. All these skills may be practiced over the full range of the continuum from therapy to social action. However, using them in the context of SDS theory leads to the addition of a further dimension in therapy. For example, learning to enhance self-esteem in a therapeutic group reflects a deficiency/pathology model typical of the traditional approach. In SDS this would take on a positive direction and become empowerment. Another example of the differences in these models might be that in the therapeutic orientation the group might be focused on sensitizing parents to children's needs. An SDS model would add a further dimension of conscientization to the rights of children. Similarly, mutual aid becomes solidarity (Breton, 1989).

CONCLUSION

This chapter offers a unifying conceptual framework for social group work and provides examples of how this model is applicable to the wide range of group work activities. Other areas such as implications for research method, or the application of theory are not explored here. It is important to note that the SDS model offers a framework for an eclectic approach which covers different theoretical approaches such as behavioral and psychodynamic, etc. It sees the goal of the group as the foremost factor to be identified in assessing the issues/problems and then requires the application of the most appropriate strategy. This frees the practitioner from being method bound (behaviorist or humanist) to becoming multi-method oriented, based on level(s) of change goals (individual to societal) in a given social situation.

Gordon (1969, p. 6) set out the criteria which he considered an integrating theory of social work should meet. It should be "consistent with . . . the enduring . . . elements of social work." It should be general enough to cover the broad variety of social work tasks and to allow for further development of the theory. It should incorporate aspects of the longer-established sciences. It should generate continued thinking and be capable of scientific evaluation.

SDS meets these broad requirements for an integrating theory. Its strength is that it avoids reductionist thinking and addresses a multi-causal analysis of social situations. It therefore advocates a multi-level/multisystem response in interventions, extending social group work to cover the range from therapy to social change.

This chapter is but an overview of the SDS model. Detailed applications and testing validity are beyond the scope of the current discussion. The authors propose that further investigations of concepts and application to practice are required to confirm the effectiveness of this global perspective of analysis and intervention for social group work education and practice.

REFERENCES

Bakalinsky, R. (1984). The small group in community organization practice. *Social Work with Groups, 7*(2), 87-96.

Bertalanffy, L. V. (1950). An outline of general systems theory. *British Journal for the Philosophy of Science, 1*, pp. 134-165.

Billups, J. D. (1984). Unifying social work: Importance of center-moving ideas. *Social Work, 29*(2), 173-180.

Billups, J. D. (1990). Towards social development as an organizing concept for social work and related social professions and movements. *Social Development Issues, 12*(3), 14-26.

Breton, M. (1989). Liberation theology group work and the right of the poor and oppressed to participate in the life of the community. *Social Work with Groups, 12*(3), 5-18.

Breton, M. (1990). Learning from social group work traditions. *Social Work with Groups, 13*(3), 21-34.

Buckley, W. (1967). *Sociology and modern systems theory.* Englewood Cliffs, NJ: Prentice Hall.

Cnaan, R. A., & Adar, H. (1987). An integrative model for group work in community organization practice. *Social Work with Groups, 10*(3), 5-24.

Conrad, P., & Schneider, J. W. (1985). *Deviance and medicalization from badness to sickness.* Columbus, OH: Merrill Publishing.

Corey, G., & Corey, M. S. (1990). *Groups: Process and practice.* Monterey, CA: Brooks/Cole.

Costin, L. B., Bell, C. J., & Downs, S. W. (1991). *Child welfare. Policies and practice* (4th ed.). New York and London: Longman.

CSWE. (1991). *Statistics on social work education.* Washington, DC: Council on Social Work Education.

Cummings, R. E. (1983). Social development: The economic, the political, and normative emphases. *International Social Work, 26*(1), 13-25.

Falk, D. R. (1981). Social development values. *Social Development Issues, 5*(1), 67-83.

Falk, D. (1984). The social development paradigm. *Social Development Issues, 8*(4), 4-14.

Fatout, M. F. (1987). Group work with severely abused and neglected latency age children: Special needs and problems. *Social Work with Groups, 10*(4), 5-19.

Feldman, R. A. (1986). Group work knowledge and research: A two-decade comparison. *Social Work with Groups, 9*(3), 7-14.

Frankel, A. J., & Sundel, M. (1978). The grope for group: Initiating individual and community change. *Social Work with Groups, 1*(4), 399-405.

Galinsky, M., Schopler, J. H., Safier, E. J., & Gambrill, E. D. (1978). Assertion training for public welfare clients. *Social Work with Groups, 1*(4), 365-379.

Garvin, C. D. (1984). The changing context of social group work practice: Challenge and opportunity. *Social Work with Groups, 7*(1), 3-19.

Gentry, M. E. (1987). Coalition formation and processes. *Social Work with Groups, 10*(3), 39-54.

Gil, D. (1981). Social policies and social development. A humanistic-egalitarian perspective. In J. F. Jones & R. S. Pandey (Eds.), *Social Development: Con-*

ceptual methodological and policy issues, (pp. 61-80). New York: St. Martin's Press.

Glasser, P. H., & Garvin, C. D. (1976). An organizational model. In R. W. Roberts & H. Northen (Eds.), *Theories of social work with groups* (Chapter 3). New York: Columbia University Press.

Glassman, U., & Kates, L. (1986). Techniques of social group work: A framework for practice. *Social Work with Groups, 9*(1), 9-38.

Gordon, W. E. (1969). Basic constructs for an integrative and generative conception of social work. In G. Hearn (Ed.), *The general systems approach: Contributions toward an holistic conception of social work* (pp. 5-11). New York: Council on Social Work Education.

Hartford, M. E. (1976). Group methods and generic practice. In R. W. Roberts & H. Northen (Eds.), *Theories of social work with groups* (Chapter 2). New York: Columbia University Press.

Hearn, G. (1969). *The general systems approach. Contributions toward an holistic conception of social work.* New York: CSWE.

Hollister, D. C. (1977). Social work skills for social development. *Social Development Issues, 1*(1), 9-19.

Jones, J. F., & Pandey, R. S. (1981). *Social development: Conceptual methodological and policy issues.* New York: St. Martin's Press.

Khinduka, S. K. (1987). Development and peace: The complex nexus. *Social Development Issues, 10*(3), 19-30.

Kuhn, T. S. (1972). *The structure of scientific revolutions,* (2nd Ed.). Chicago, IL: University of Chicago Press.

Leighninger, R. D. (1977). Systems theory and social work: A re-examination. *Journal of Education for Social Work, 13*(3), 44-69.

Leonard, P. (1975). Towards a paradigm for racial practice. In R. Bailey & M. Brake (Eds.), *Radical social work* (Chapter 3). New York: Pantheon Books.

Lieberman, M. A. (1975). Group methods. In F. H. Kanfer & A. P. Goldstein (Eds.), *Helping People Change* (Chapter 13). New York: Pergamon Press.

Maier, H. W. (1981). Models of intervention in work with groups: Which is yours? *Social Group Work, 4*(3,4), 21-36.

Mayadas, N. S., & Duehn, W. (1986). Video-stimulus-modeling methodology: A format for leadership training in social work with groups. In P. H. Glasser & N. S. Mayadas (Eds.), *Group Workers at Work: Theory and Practice in the 80s.* Totowa, NJ: Rowman & Littlefield, pp. 250-264.

Mayadas, N. S., & Glasser, P. H. (1986). The changing nature of social group work practice. In P. H. Glasser & N. S. Mayadas (Eds.), *Group Workers at Work: Theory and Practice in the 80s.* Totowa, NJ: Rowman & Littlefield, pp. 3-8.

Meinert, R., Kohn, E., & Strickler, G. (1984). International survey of social development concepts. *Social Development Issues, 8*(1-2), 70-88.

Meinert, R., & Kohn, E. (1987). Towards operationalization of social development concepts. *Social Development Issues, 10*(3), 4-18.

Meyer, C. (1990). Repairing our fractured profession. *Columbia University Alumni Newsletter,* (Fall/Winter), 2-3.

Middleman, R. R., & Wood, G. G. (1990a). *Skills for direct practice in social work.* New York: Columbia University Press.

Middleman, R. R., & Wood, G. G. (1990b). From social group work to social work with groups. *Social Work with Groups, 13*(3), 3-20.

Midgley, J. (1984a). Social welfare implications of development paradigms. *Social Service Review, 58*(2), 181-198.

Midgley, J. (1984b). Social work services in the third world: Towards the integration of remedial and developmental orientations. *Social Development Issues, 8*(1), 89-104.

Omer, S. (1979). Social development. *International Social Work,* XXII(3), 11-26.

Paiva, J. F. X. (1977). A conception of social development. *Social Service Review, 51*(2), 327-336.

Papell, C., & Rothman, B. (1966). Social group work models: possession and heritage. *Journal of Education for Social Work, 2*(2), 66-77.

Reeser, L. C., & Leighninger, L. (1990). Back to our roots: Towards a specialization in social justice. *Journal of Sociology and Social Welfare, 17*(2), 69-87.

Rose, S. M. (1990). Advocacy/empowerment: An approach to clinical practice for social work. *Journal of Sociology and Social Welfare, 17*(2), 41-51.

Rubin, A., & Johnson, P. J. (1984). Direct practice interests of entering MSW students. *Journal of Education for Social Work,* 20, 5-16.

Saleeby, D. (1990). Philosophical disputes in social work: Social justice denied. *Journal of Sociology and Social Welfare, 27*(2), 29-39.

Sanders, D. S. (1987). The developmental perspective in social work. *Indian Journal of Social Work,* XLVII(4), 379-388.

Seidman, E. (1983). *Handbook of social intervention.* Beverly Hills, CA: Sage Publications.

Shaffer, J. B. P., & Galinsky, D. H. (1974). *Models of group therapy and sensitivity training.* Englewood Cliffs, NJ: Prentice Hall.

Shulman, L. (1969). Social systems theory in field instruction: A case example. In G. Hearn (Ed.), *The general systems approach: Contributions toward an holistic conception of social work.* New York: CSWE.

Silverman, M. (1966). Knowledge in social group work: A review of the literature. *Social Work, 11*(3), 56-62.

Specht, H. (1990). Social work and the popular psychotherapies, *Social Service Review, 64*(3), 345-357.

Spergel, I. A. (1977). Social development and social work. *Administration in social work, 1*(3), 221-233.

Swartz, S., & Dattalo, P. (1990). Factors affecting student selection of macro specializations. *Administration in social work, 14*(3), 83-96.

Tropp, E. (1976). A developmental theory. In R. W. Roberts & H. Northen (Eds.), *Theories of social work with groups* (Chapter 7). New York: Columbia University Press.

Wakefield, J. C. (1988a). Psychotherapy, distributive justice and social work, Part I. Distributive justice as a conceptual framework for social work. *Social Service Review, 62*(2), 187-210.

Wakefield, J. C. (1988b). Psychotherapy, distributive justice and social work, Part II. Psychotherapy and the pursuit of justice. *Social Service Review, 62*(3), 354-382.

Wilson, G. (1976). From practice to theory: A personalized history. In R. W. Roberts & H. Northen (Eds.), *Theories of social work with groups* (Chapter 1). New York: Columbia University Press.

Chapter 8

Group Work with Children of Substance Abusers: Beyond the Basics

MaryAnn Hosang

BACKGROUND

One in every ten adults in the United States is a problem drinker (Seixas & Youcha, 1985), and 73% of them are married (Ackerman, 1986, p. ix). The result is 6.6 million children of substance abusers (COSAs) under age 18 (National Institute on Alcohol Abuse and Alcoholism, 1990), or one in every four school children (*Living With Parents Who Drink Too Much*, 1990). Fifty percent of the children who grow up in a chemically addicted home will become substance abusers themselves if intervention is not made (Cotton, 1989). In addition, COSAs score lower on intelligence tests (Gabrielli & Mednic, 1983); they have more difficulties in school (Johnson & Rolf, 1988) and are more likely to drop out of school (Moe & Pohlman, 1989); and they are more depressed and anxious than other children (Johnson & Rolf, 1988). Finally, COSAs are much more likely to enter the juvenile justice system; are more prone to experience psychological difficulties than other children (National Institute on Alcohol Abuse and Alcoholism, 1990); are at high risk for becoming overachieving, pregnant, addicted, or codependent; suicide; and experiencing stress-related problems (Moe & Pohlman, 1989).

What factors within an addicted home contribute to the much higher incidence of problems among the children? Young children living with substance abusing parents (COSAs) are attempting to cope with volatile, chaotic, and unpredictable environments. The home that is headed by an alcoholic or addict is typified by five conditions, as described by Charles Deutsch (1982). These conditions include centricity of the chemically dependent persons and their behaviors; denial and shame; inconsistency, insecurity, and fear; anger and hatred; and guilt and blame. In other words, the family system revolves around the addiction; constantly attempting to maintain equilibrium in the face of erratic behavior, all the while pretending there isn't an addictive problem, and blaming anything and everything else for the misery within the family. The children in such a system learn to keep silent about the addiction and to simply pretend nothing is wrong.

Besides producing a chaotic system, addicted parents are usually impaired in their ability to provide role stability, environmental consistency, dependability, and emotional availability. The children learn to cope by becoming psuedo-adult, over-dependent, oppositional, manipulative, withdrawn, or otherwise display poor interpersonal skills (Morehouse & Richards, 1986). Although these interpersonal adjustments work very well within the home, they don't translate well in the world at large. In fact, these children are quite often experiencing major social, academic, or behavioral problems in settings outside the home.

In addition, many children of chemically dependent mothers were exposed to drugs or alcohol *in utero*, which very often negatively affects their learning and behavioral capacities. There are 24,000 births each year that are identified as Fetal Alcohol Syndrome (FAS) (Gress, 1988). However, it is a fallacy that all children affected by FAS exhibit the obvious physical features and mental retardation associated with the syndrome; an additional 36,000 infants each year are identified as having Fetal Alcohol Effects (FAE), a milder form of the syndrome. In fact, many children who appear normal in appearance and intelligence at birth have been adversely impacted by prenatal exposure to chemicals, and the impact is not noticed until much later and thus are not included in these figures (Little & Ervin, 1984). Further, the mothers tend to minimize when reporting their prenatal chemical use, making diagnosis speculative at best. Typically, these children lack the imagination to associate their actions with possible consequences in the future, and have extremely poor impulse control (Little & Ervin, 1984). Often, children thus affected are mislabeled as a "behavior problem," and it is assumed that they could behave appropriately if the consequences are made more severe. The long-term result of this downward spiral is escalation of the negative behaviors as the children become increasingly angry and frustrated as adults become increasingly punitive. By the time the children are referred for treatment, they have often become hostile and suspicious of all authority, and their self-esteem and locus of control have suffered tremendously.

Add another factor to this mix of interpersonal, intrapersonal, and physiological problems: parents who are going to be suspicious of outside interference and uninvested in their children's improvement. Chemically dependent parents are notorious for inaccurate reporting, denial, blame, and inconsistency of involvement in treatment for their children (Morehouse & Richards, 1986). In addition, the family system may be very invested in keeping the children problematic, since the children can then be blamed for the family's unhappiness, taking the focus off the addiction (Kinney & Leaton, 1987).

In the past several years, there has been a dramatic movement in the United States to provide services to children living in chemically dependent homes. A myriad of curricula have been developed that are designed to provide education, emotional support, and alternative coping skills in small support group settings. Most of these curricula can be facilitated by a compassionate lay person who has some special training in the specific curriculum. In support groups, children learn about the dynamics of addiction, emphasizing that the addiction is a disease over which the child has no control. Other topics for support group sessions include problem-solving skills, appropriate expression of feelings, and assertiveness. Support groups are also valuable because the COSAs discover that there are lots of other children in the same predicament, and realize that they can help themselves and each other. Support groups are appropriate and helpful for COSAs who have manifested minimal emotional or behavioral problems, and just need some basic information and peer support.

BEYOND THE BASICS

Obviously, a support group that follows a specific curriculum and is facilitated by a nonprofessional is a very valuable experience to any child in a substance-abusing home, but most COSAs are in need of so much more than simply education and support. Clearly, those COSAs with emotional and/or behavioral problems are at even higher risk to develop chemical dependency problems later in life than the more resilient children. For the majority of COSAs, a therapeutic and systemic intervention is more appropriate. Therapeutic groups have a slightly different structure and very different methods than a support group, and facilitation is by a trained therapist.

Facilitation

According to Jerry Moe (July 25, 1989), the minimal requirements of a competent COSA group therapist include expertise in child development, *and* expertise in substance abuse, *and* expertise in therapy skills. The COSA therapist must be flexible, consistent, creative, and patient. Further, the therapist must be able to set safe, consistent limits and possess excellent listening skills (Moe, July 25, 1989). Perhaps most important, the COSA therapist must have already worked through his/her own childhood issues, and have a support system outside of work. Once COSAs truly trust the group, they are painfully honest and graphic about the things they see, hear, and experience. Their issues can easily trigger counter-transference which can hinder the therapeutic process.

Family Intervention

In my years of experience with COSA families, I have come to realize that, although addicted people make lousy parents, not one of them wants to be a bad parent. They do the very best they can with the tools they have. Unfortunately, most dysfunctional adults had dysfunctional parents themselves, and thus have limited information about how to parent. Added to the everyday challenges of attempting to parent "in the dark" are the stresses of addiction, finances, and the struggle to appear normal to the outside world in the midst of chaos. It is a small wonder that addicted families are often overwhelmed with life!

The Social Worker has many opportunities for intervention within the family. Providing parenting support can make a powerful impact on the family. These families also need an advocate, someone to help them work with the schools and community to meet the special needs of their children. Further, many addicted homes are also in need of linkages with other agencies including basic commodities such as food, shelter, utilities, and medical attention.

Surrogate Role Models

In a longitudinal study, Werner (1986) discovered that although many children of substance abusers develop problems, some don't. Werner studied those children who were resilient, looking for the common characteristics that resilient children share that may have contributed to their success. Receiving positive attention from other people figured prominently, usually from a surrogate parenting figure. Other research supports this finding (Wolin & Wolin, 1993). An important part of a comprehensive COSA program should include a "Big Brother/ Big Sister" type program that matches COSAs with an adult who has been specifically drained in chemical dependency issues and communication skills. Hays Caldwell Council on Alcohol and Drug Abuse in San Marcos, Texas, developed a "Big Buddy" program which has made a dramatic impact on many young COSAs, enhancing their self-esteem, communication skills, and self-expression skills. This kind of program requires careful screening and training, thoughtful matching, and a great deal of follow-up contact, but the results have been rewarding. Coordination of a quality surrogate parenting program of fifteen matches occupies a great deal of time, and it may be advisable to recruit manpower to assist.

SUMMARY

Although curriculum-based support groups meet some of the needs of children of substance abusers, they fall short of serving

COSAs comprehensively. These children need so much more than simply education and support if they are to grow up drug free. They also need therapeutic intervention, family intervention, and advocation by a professional trained to provide all three. Social workers are well prepared to handle the challenge of providing comprehensive services to these children and their families, helping resolve issues today to prevent problems later.

BIBLIOGRAPHY

Ackerman, R. J. (1986). *Growing in the Shadow,* pg. ix. Health Communications, Popano Beach, FL.

Cotton, N. S. (1979). The Familial Incidence of Alcoholism. *Journal of Studies on Alcohol.* 40: pp. 89-116.

Deutsch, C. (1982). *Broken Bottles, Broken Dreams.* Teachers College Press, Columbia University, NY.

Gabrielli, W. F. & Mednic, S. A. (1983). Intellectual performance in children of alcoholics. *Journal of Nervous and Mental Disease 171.*

Gress, J. R. (1988). Alcoholism's hidden curriculum. *Student Assistance Journal, N/D.*

Johnson, J. & Rolf, J. E. (1988). Cognitive functioning in children from alcoholic and nonalcoholic families. *Journal of Addictions 83.*

Kinney, J. and Leaton, G. (1987). *Loosening the Grip: A Handbook of Alcohol Information.* Times Mirror/Mosby College Publishing, St. Louis.

Little, R. & Ervin, C. (1984). Alcohol use and reproduction, in Wilsnack & Beckman, eds., *Alcohol Problems in Women,* Guilford Press.

Living with Parents Who Drink Too Much. (1990). Van Nuys, California: Aims Media. Video.

Moe, J. & Pohlman, D. (1989). *Kids' Power: Healing Games for Children of Alcoholics.* HCI, Popano Beach, FL.

Moe, J. (1989). Group skills in assisting young children of substance abusers. Workshop at: *Texas Commission on Alcohol and Drug Abuse: 32nd Annual Institute of Drug Studies,* July 25.

Morehouse, E. R. & Richards, T. (1986). An examination of dysfunctional latency age children of alcoholic parents and problems in intervention. In Ackerman, ed, *Growing in the Shadow.* Health Communications, Inc., Popano Beach, FL.

National Institute on Alcohol Abuse and Alcoholism. (1990). Children of alcoholics: Are they different? In *Alcohol Alert, 9.*

Seixas, J. S. & Youcha, G. (1985). *Children of Alcoholism: A Survivor's Manual.* Crown, NY.

Werner, E. E. (1986). Resilient offspring of alcoholics: A longitudinal study from birth to age 18. *Journal of Studies on Alcohol 47(1).*

Wolin, S. J. and Wolin, S. W. (1993). *The Resilient Self.* Villard Books, NY.

Chapter 9

Utilizing a Group Approach to Improve the Social Skills of Children with Learning Disabilities

Juanita B. Hepler

Peer relations are an important part of the socialization process of the child and require the utilization of many complex skills. These interactions play a major and unique role in the child's ability to interact with others, to develop social control, and incorporate social values (Hartup, 1983; Berndt, Caparulo, McCartney, and Moore, 1980). Positive peer interactions are also related to the child's emotional security and involvement with the environment (Hartup, 1983).

Negative consequences for those children who are rejected by peers include behavioral and academic problems in school. These children are more likely to be truant, repeat grade levels, and drop out of school (Parker and Asher, 1987; Kupersmidt, 1983; Ullman, 1957). In a longitudinal, Kupersmidt (1983) found almost half of the rejected children were retained or repeated a grade level at least once over the six-year period. There is a strong correlation between negative interactions with peer and juvenile delinquency (Parker and Asher, 1987; Kupersmidt, 1983). Further evidence suggests that adults with adjustment and psychological problems (including job and marriage adjustment) experienced difficulties in their peer relationships as children (Ginsberg, Gottman, and Parker, 1986; Parker and Asher, 1987). This was highlighted in a study conducted by Cowen et al., (1973) which found that peer ratings were a stronger predictor of adult adjustment than several variables including scholastic achievement and aptitude and self-esteem.

Peer relations and children with learning disabilities. Children with developmental disabilities are at risk for experiencing problems in their social interactions with peers. They exhibit behavioral and cognitive deficits in their peer relationships and consistently receive low ratings on sociometric measures indicating that they have low social status (Silver and Young, 1985; Ray, 1985; Taylor, Asher, and Williams, 1987). In addition, nonhandicapped children may take control and play more adult roles when they interact with handicapped peers. Thus the interactions tend to involve adult to child interactions rather than child to child. This means the handicapped child may have fewer opportunities to learn and use peer related skills based on equal interactions (Guralnick, 1986).

As a group, children with learning disabilities experience the negative peer relations previously described for children with developmental disabilities. They have low social status (Kistner and Gatlin, 1989; Hepler, 1991), and this rejection may begin at a very early age. Vaughen et al., (1990) examined the peer relations of children during their first two months in kindergarten. They found 60% of the learning disabled (LD) children in their study had low social status and none had high status. While some studies report that LD children use more negative behaviors, there is no conclusive evidence that these children use significantly different behavior patterns. In fact, rather than using negative behaviors, LD children appear to be more conforming in their social interactions. They do seem to experience problems with cognitive skills and have greater difficulty interpreting or being sensitive to the nonverbal behaviors of peers. In addition, LD children's self-perceptions concerning their social competence and status tend to be inflated (Hepler, 1991; Vaughen et al., 1990). Problems in cognitive development are probably related to their shorter attention span and off-task behavior which contributes to their low social status (Vaughen et al., 1990; Bryan and Bryan, 1983).

Many adults, including parents and teachers, seem to have lower expectations for LD children both in their social and academic performance. Several studies report that mothers of LD children give less positive reinforcement and use more negative statements than parents of NLD children (McKinney, 1979; Bryan, Donahue, Pearl, and Herzog, 1981; Bryan and Bryan, 1983). Teachers also rate these children as using more negative inappropriate behaviors including poor social skills (Bryan and Bryan, 1983).

These studies indicate that LD children receive more negative behaviors and less positive reinforcement both from peers and adults. While the LD child may exhibit certain academic deficits related to their disability, it does not mean they cannot perform well in other academic areas; however, the lower expectations from both parents and teachers may have a negative impact on their performance. Likewise, rejection by peers, and less positive reinforcement from adults would make it difficult for LD children to overcome skill deficits and engage in positive interactions with peers.

In response to these problems, mainstreaming was viewed as a very promising method to improve not only the academic performance of LD children, but also to improve their social environment by providing an opportunity for these children to interact with nonhandicapped students. According to Gresham (1982) the high expectations for mainstreaming were based on three faulty assumptions: (1) it would increase positive social interactions between handicapped and nonhandicapped children, (2) handicapped children would experience greater acceptance, and (3) handicapped children would model the behaviors of their nonhandicapped cohorts. As he points out, there is little evidence to indicate that these three assumptions have occurred when children with developmental disabilities have been mainstreamed. Instead, nonhandicapped children tend to interact with other nonhandicapped children, and handicapped children have not experienced greater acceptance (skill deficits and the use of inappropriate or negative behaviors may contribute to the lack of integration between the two groups). Nor have children with handicaps routinely modeled the behaviors of nonhandicapped children, because many lack the basic cognitive and behavioral skills to imitate the behaviors of others. Therefore, rather than helping the handicapped child, mainstreaming may, in fact, contribute to further rejection and isolation (Gresham, 1982). Certainly, the lack of acceptance by peers and the more negative attitudes of teachers does not make for an accepting environment for these children.

It is clear that LD children will need assistance if mainstreaming is to be a positive experience for them. Social skills programs can be beneficial, but it is essential that these programs also work with the NLD children, because little change can occur for the LD child without a change in the negative behaviors and attitudes of NLD children. This article discusses the implementation of a social skills program designed to improve the social skills of LD children and to improve their social interactions with their NLD cohorts.

SOCIAL SKILLS PROGRAM FOR LD CHILDREN

Information concerning the social interactions of children, including children with learning disabilities, provides important guidelines for developing effective social skill interventions for LD children. First, social interactions become more complex as the child moves from preschool through adolescence (Dodge et al., 1986; Coie and Dodge, 1983); therefore, programs need to be aware of and emphasize age-appropriate skills. As previously mentioned, an effective program must also address the negative attitudes that NLD children have concerning LD children.

Sample. The present study involved two "regular" fifth grade classrooms (n = 26) and two fifth grade special education classes (n = 15). The special education classrooms included LD children who required additional academic and support resources. These children were mainstreamed into regular academic classrooms whenever possible but spent the majority of each day in the special education classrooms. The children (ages 10-12 years) came from predominantly white, working class families. All children in the two special education classrooms participated in the program. Teachers from the regular classrooms were asked to select up to fifteen students who were socially accepted by classmates. Several studies have shown that teachers are able to make reasonably accurate assessments of the social status of their students (La Greca, 1981). Parental consent was obtained for all students who participated in the study.

One regular and one special education classroom (n=22) were randomly assigned to the treatment group (TG) and received the social skills training (LD:8 boys, 1 girl; NLD:8 boys, 5 girls). The remaining regular and special education classroom (n = 19) were assigned to the control group (CG) and were tested at pre, post, and follow-up in order to assess the impact of the intervention (LD:6 girls, 0 boys; NLD:11 boys, 2 girls). Children in the treatment group were randomly assigned to small training groups (n = 4-5) with the stipulation that each group included both boys and girls, LD and NLD students, and high and low status children. Group composition was designed to provide an opportunity for boys and girls, LD and NLD, and high and low status children to interact and develop new friendships in a safe, structured setting.

Format. Children learned behavioral, cognitive, and affective skills. Based on earlier studies demonstrating their relationship to social acceptance, the following behavioral skills were included in the program: (1) initiating and maintaining a conversation, (2) including others, (3) entering an ongoing activity, (4) responding to negative behaviors from peers. Cognitive skills included the problem-solving steps, another important component of positive social status (Dodge et al., 1986). These steps include the ability to: (1) identify the problem, (2) list possible alternative solutions and consequences, (3) select and implement the most effective solution decision. The affective component focused on children's self-perceptions concerning social interactions (Wheeler and Ladd, 1982; Sobol and Earn, 1985). Children with low social status tend to feel they have little control over their social environment and that the environment is stable or unchanging. In the program we emphasize that the student has control and responsibility for what occurs in social interactions and that the social environment is changeable. We stress that using appropriate social behaviors will result in more positive interactions. However, because low status children are frequently rejected even when they use the correct behaviors, we point out that the fault does not lie with the individual if he or she has made several positive attempts to engage in positive interactions. In this situation the responsibility lies with the other persons.

The use of small groups is the major forum to bring about changes in the social network patterns. Within these groups, LD and NLD children work together to learn and practice new skills. Trained group leaders (school social workers and psychologists) utilize activities that encourage interactions across gender, status and disability. There is a major emphasis on developing "group spirit" and working together to accomplish group goals. The last fifteen minutes of each session are used for recreational activities that provide another opportunity for children to interact. It also helps to make meetings "fun" and promotes the development of group cohesion. Friendships developed within these small groups can be generalized beyond this setting to the classroom and larger school environment.

Students meet for one hour once a week for eight weeks. Each session focuses on one of the previously described behavioral skills with students using the problem-solving steps to develop solutions. The group leader emphasizes internal control and that the social environment can be modified when we use appropriate behaviors. The group leader begins each session by discussing a problem situation and then leads the students through the problem-solving steps in order to develop an effective solution. Specific steps are outlined (one of the four behavioral skills previously discussed) and students use roleplaying and feedback to rehearse the skill. Homework sheets are issued which list the specific steps, and students are instructed to use the skill in a social situation at school during the following week. They complete the homework sheets and bring them to the following session for discussion and evaluation. This promotes generalization of learned skills to the outside environment.

Students receive tokens for completing homework assignments and participating in discussion and roleplays. Group members are encouraged to work together in order to earn the required number of tokens for a pizza party at the last session (group goal). Again this helps to promote group cohesion.

Measures. Several measures were used to assess the effectiveness of the program. Sociometric ratings and nominations were used to examine the social status of students. On the rating scale, students were asked to indicate how much they liked to play with fellow classmates (all students within their treatment condition). A scale of 1-5 was used with a 1 indicating they did not like to play with the individual and a 5 indicating they liked to play with the student a lot. Children were asked to list 0-3 students that were favorite playmates for positive nominations and a rating of 1 was used for negative nominations (for ethical reasons students were not asked to list students they did not like to play with). Observational data assessed behaviors and the gender, disability, and status of peers that each child interacted with during free play periods. A self-perception measure, The Children's Self-Efficacy for Social Interactions With Peers Scale (CPSI) was administered to assess student's perceptions of their social competence in using verbal skills. This measure asked students to indicate how difficult it would be for them to use specific verbalizations in conflict and nonconflict situations. Students also completed a program evaluation measure which asked them to assess their enjoyment of the program, if they made new friends, if they felt the skills emphasized in the program were relevant, and if they planned to use these skills.

OUTCOME AND DISCUSSION

When we implemented this program, we did not know how well the LD and NLD children would work together. There was the possibility that the NLD children would not enjoy participating in the groups and would express a desire to withdraw from the program (all students were free to withdraw from the program at any time). On the other hand, there was also the possibility that the LD children would be uncomfortable in the small groups and exhibit low levels of participation during the sessions or even fail to attend. Happily neither of these scenarios occurred, and all children in the treatment group completed the eight sessions. The NLD children did not register negative complaints, and the LD children were active participants. This positive outcome was probably the result of the specific structure of the program which included group goals, fun activities, and the expertise of the group leaders who encouraged participation and made certain that a safe environment was maintained where children could experiment with and practice new behaviors. The response from the LD teacher was also very positive. She felt her students had learned valuable skills and was enthusiastic about further participation in the program.

The students in the treatment group completed an evaluation of the program during session eight. Results showed that the majority of the students found the sessions to be very enjoyable and fun. They felt they made new friends, and they liked some group members and classmates better after participating in the program. Overall, students indicated that they felt the skills they learned were important, that the steps were relevant, and that they planned to use these new skills at least some of the time. This measure provides important information for improving the social skills program. For example, we can determine which skills seemed most important and relevant to students. Negative feedback would indicate we need to make changes in the program if we want to be effective in working with students.

Sociometric measures indicated positive changes in the attitudes and social status of students. We examined the combined *ratings* of all LD and NLD students within treatment conditions and also looked at the *ratings* made by LD children only and NLD students only. An examination of scores (pre, post, and follow-up) showed that in the treatment group all three groups (LD and NLD combined, LD only, NLD only) gave modest ratings at pretest, higher ratings at posttest and small decreases at follow-up (five months). Scores for the control group followed a somewhat different pattern. The combined LD and NLD ratings and LD ratings only, showed relatively high scores at pretest; NLD children gave more modest ratings. The combined NLD and LD, and LD only gave lower ratings at posttest with large decreases at follow-up. NLD children showed improvement at posttest and a decrease at follow-up. A preliminary analyses showed that the ratings for all three groups (NLD and LD, NLD, LD) were significantly higher for the treatment group when compared to the no treatment control group (statistical outcome will be discussed in a later article).

These scores suggest that children in the treatment group made positive gains as a result of participating in the social skills program. The small decreases at follow-up indicate that some of these positive attitudes were maintained five months later. On the other hand, children in the control seemed to experience more negative feelings toward one another over time. Only one group (NLD) experienced a small increase at posttest and all three groups showed decreases in ratings at follow-up. It should be noted that both the treatment and control groups were observed during free play periods at posttest only. Within treatment conditions, children participated in free play activities for 30 minutes over a six-week period. This heightened exposure for children in the control group without the added structure of the social skills program may have increased the negative feelings both LD and NLD children had for one another. The results on the sociometric ratings also highlight the difficulty LD children encounter when they attempt to interact with NLD children. The scores for the treatment group indicate that it was the NLD children who experienced the smallest gains in developing more positive accepting attitudes toward peers.

A preliminary examination of the observational data showed LD children in the treatment group interacting with high status students and spending less time with other low status children. This may reflect a change in the traditional social network which shows LD children isolated from NLD peers. Comparison to the control group is problematic because the LD children in the control group were girls and many of the high status students are boys. This would make it very difficult for control group children to change social networks as fifth grade students tend to interact with same sex peers. No major changes were noted in the CPSI measure, primarily because many LD children had relatively high scores at pretest.

SUMMARY

Mainstreaming is viewed as a positive step for improving the academic and social functioning of LD children. However, NLD students exhibit negative attitudes toward LD children and frequently exclude them for social activities. Teachers may also use less positive reinforcement with LD children. Consequently, mainstreaming may expose these children to a more hostile and isolated environment. Developing effective training programs for teachers and students can help to bring about positive change for the social development of LD children. Social skills programs that promote skill acquisition along with the modification of the negative attitudes of NLD children have taken a major step to improve the peer relations of these children and to foster their integration into society.

REFERENCES

Berndt, T. J., Caparulo, B., McCartney, K., and Moore, A. (1980). Processes and outcomes of social influence in children's peer groups. Unpublished manuscript, Yale University.

Bryan, J. H. and Bryan, T. H. (1983). The social life of the learning disabled youngster, in *Current Topics in Learning Disabilities*, J. D. McKinney, L. Feagans (Eds.). New Jersey: Ablex Publishing Corporation, 57-80.

Bryan, T., Donahue, M. Pearl, R., and Herzog, A. (1981). Learning disabled children-mother interactions during a problem solving task. Unpublished manuscript, Northwestern University.

Coie, J. D. and Dodge, K. A. (1983). Continuities and changes in children's social status: A five-year longitudinal study, *Merrill Palmer Quarterly*, 29, 261-282.

Cowen, E., Pederson, A., Babijian, H., Izzo, L. and Troust, M. (1973). Long-term follow-up of early detected vulnerable children, *Journal of Consulting and Clinical Psychology*, 41, 438-466.

Dodge, K., Pettit, G., McClaskey, C., and Brown, M. (1986). Social competence in children. *Monographs of the Society for Research in Child Development*, 51(2).

Ginsberg, D., Gottman, J. M., and Parker, J. G. (1986). The importance of friendship, in *Conversations of Friends, Speculations on Affective Development*. J. M. Gottman and J. G. Parker (Eds.). New York: Cambridge University Press, 3-50.

Gresham, F. M. (1982). Misguided mainstreaming: The case for social skills training with handicapped children, *Exceptional Children*, Vol. 49(5), 422-431.

Guralnick, M. J. (1986). The peer relations of young handicapped and nonhandicapped children. *Children's Social Behavior: Development, Assessment, and Modification*. P. S. Strain, M. J. Guralnick, and H. M. Walker (Eds.). New York: Academic Press, Inc., 93-139.

Hartup, W. (1983). Peer relations. In E. M. Hetherington (Eds.) *Psychopathology and Child Development*. New York: Wiley, 103-174.

Hepler, J. B. (1991). An examination of the social status of fifth grade children with learning disabilities. Manuscript submitted for publication.

Kistner, J. A. and Gatlin, D. F. (1989). Sociometric differences between learning disabled and nonhandicapped students: Effects of sex and race, *Journal of Educational Psychology*, 81(1), 118-120.

Kupersmidt J. (1983). Predicting delinquency and academic problems from childhood peer status. Paper presented at the Biennial Meeting of the Society for Research in Child Development, Detroit, MI.

La Greca, A. M. (1981). Peer acceptance: The correspondence between children's sociometric scores and teacher's ratings of peer interactions, *Journal of Abnormal Child Psychology*, 9, 167-178.

McKinney, J. D. (1979). Families of learning disabled children. Paper presented at the meeting of the North Carolina Association for Learning Disabilities.

Parker, J. and Asher, S. (1987). Peer relations and later personal adjustment: Are low-accepted children at risk?, *Psychological Bulletin*, 102(3), 356-389.

Ray, B. M. (1985). Measuring the social position of the mainstreamed handicapped child, *Exceptional Children*, 52(1), 57-62.

Silver, D. S. and Young, R. D. (1985). Interpersonal problem-solving abilities, peer status and behavioral adjustment in learning disabled and nonlearning disabled adolescents, *Advances in Learning and Behavioral Disabilities*, 4, 201-223.

Sobol, M. P. and Earn, B. M. (1985). Assessment of children's attributions for social experiences: Implications for social skills training. In B. H. Schneider, K. H. Rubin & J. E. Ledingham (Eds.), *Children's peer relations: Issues in assessment and intervention.* New York: Springer-Verlag, 93-101.

Taylor, A. R., Asher, S. R., and Williams, G. A. (1987). The social adaptation of mainstreamed mildly retarded children, *Child Development,* 58, 1321-1334.

Ullman, C. (1957). Teachers, peers, and tests as predictors of adjustment, *The Journal of Educational Psychology,* 48:257-267.

Vaughen, S., Hogan, A., Kouzekanani, K., and Shapiro, S. (1990). Peer acceptance, self-perceptions, and social skills of learning disabled students prior to identification, *Journal of Educational Psychology,* 82(1), 101-106.

Wheeler, V. A. and Ladd, G. W. (1982). Assessment of Children's Self-Efficacy for Social Interactions with Peers, *Developmental Psychology,* 18(6), 795-805.

Chapter 10

The Use of Self
in Group Work:
Power and Empowerment

Hisashi Hirayama
Kasumi K. Hirayama

INTRODUCTION

The topic of this chapter is "The Use of Self in Group Work: Power and Empowerment." But first we would like to tell you why we became interested in this subject.

Some of our Japanese colleagues who have come to know American society and American social work are at times amused by Americans' interest and emphasis on the importance of "power" in society and in interpersonal relationships: political power, economic power, black power, white power, women's power, elderly power, and so forth.

In Japanese, the word power generally evokes more or less negative images in the listener's mind, as the word "power" equates with "kenryoku" or authoritative and autocratic forces which exert control over people and their life space. Thus the word provokes such emotions as anger, anxiety, fear, threat, and resistance in the minds of hearers. However, the negative connotation placed on the word "power" by the Japanese does not mean that they are unaware of the existence or use of power in interpersonal relationships. The noted existential analyst Rollo May (1972) says, "for the living person, power is not a theory but an ever-present reality which must confront, use, enjoy, and struggle with a hundred times a day" (p. 100). But one difference between Americans and Japanese is that while Americans, just as May (1972) has said, "confront, use, enjoy and struggle" with power openly, Japanese tend to avoid, deny, and shun the open use of power in daily living. If power is used, it is used covertly, behind the scenes.

We think that Americans' open power-consciousness is attributed to several characteristics in American society. American society, first of all, emphasizes the importance of individuality and individualism, and the society functions on a free-market ideology. In a free-market system, competition, not cooperation, is a basic ingredient for survival, achievement, and success. How one uses his power, control, and influence to get ahead becomes one of the major concerns among Americans. Thus, in a combination of free-market ideology and individualism, fostering a competitive spirit in the child is an important educational goal for many parents. Becoming independent and self-sufficient from an early age on is always something to be encouraged, practiced, and reinforced. Individualism, not groupness, is a foundation of American ideology. Dependence or even interdependence is not a desirable quality in the American personality.

In reviewing the recent professional literature, we have come to notice new paradigms, such as the second-order cybernetics and social constructionist theory in the field of family therapy (Anderson and Goolishian, 1988; Griffith, Griffith, and Slovik, 1990; Hoffman, 1990; Real, 1990; Varela, 1989), and the membership perspective (Falck, 1989) in social group work. These new paradigms appear not only to suggest a departure from "old" and traditional views of family/group as a living system, but also a new way of viewing a family/group as a system of relationships. Naturally, these paradigms suggest significant changes in the roles and functions of the therapist/worker in relation to members of the family/group and the family/group as a whole. One of the central issues in this paradigmatic change is "power," in particular, the use of power by the therapist/worker in his effort to achieve therapeutic goals. Thus, for all the reasons above, we set out to examine or, better, to re-examine the concept of power in light of the new paradigms, its implications for client's empowerment, and also to explicate the worker's use of self (power) in social work with groups.

THE DEFINITION OF POWER AND EMPOWERMENT

Webster's (1982) dictionary offers several definitions of power. But at least two of the definitions appear most relevant to social work. One is "the ability to do or act; capability of doing or accomplishing something" and the other is "the possession of control or command over others; authority; ascendancy." In social work and its related fields, power is defined as "the ability or capacity to act or perform effectively (Pernell, 1985) or "the ability to cause or prevent change" (May, 1972).

The word "empower" is defined by Webster's (1982) as "to give power or authority to; to give ability to; enable; permit." This definition assumes the act of power being given to someone by someone else. In social work, empowerment is defined as "the capacity to influence the forces which affect one's life space for one's own and others' benefit" (Pernell, 1985) or most recently is defined by Parsons (1991) as "the process of gaining power, developing power, taking or seizing power, or facilitating or enabling power."

In the social work literature, the concept of power is used essentially in two different ways. One of the functions of power is the person's ability or capacity for adaptation–the continuous active efforts of humans to reach a goodness-of-fit with their environment (Germain, 1979). Coping, the function of adaptation, is the expression of our power over the environment in order to control, organize, and integrate ourselves and the environment for survival, security, and equilibrium. This explanation appears akin to the common purpose of social work practice and does not seem to present any controversy among practicing social workers. However, the other way of applying the concept of power has to do with the worker's conscious use of authority, status, and expertise in order to achieve goals by manipulating the client and environment for change. The use of this kind of power by the worker appears to invite disagreements and controversies among social workers, as it creates ethical dilemmas in view of the professional values such as "client self-determination" in the worker.

THE ISSUE OF POWER IN FAMILY THERAPY

Currently a debate is going on among family therapy theoreticians about the use of power by the therapist for therapeutic purposes. To summarize this debate, the proponents of power are represented by such noted theoreticians as Milton Erickson and Jay Haley who believe that power is central to all human relationships. Haley has portrayed human relationships as an ongoing struggle for status and control. Furthermore, he describes the practice of therapy as a set of maneuvers, strategies, and countermaneuvers between therapist and client as each seeks to control the other. The directive, power-oriented therapy that was created by Erickson and Haley is today called "strategic therapy."

At the other extreme, Gregory Bateson (1972) claims that power is a lineal epistemologically incorrect idea that is completely inconsistent with the systemic view. Furthermore, he insists that belief in "the validity of the metaphor of power in human relations" would ultimately and always be destructive (Dell, 1989). Bateson (1972) says:

> I think–that there is no area in which false premises regarding the nature of the self and its relations to others can be so surely productive of destruction and ugliness as this area of ideas about control. (p. 267)

Thus, for Bateson, belief in "the myth of power" is an error in thinking–rather than a fundamental aspect of human existence as it is for Haley.

Furthermore, the so-called second-order family therapists such as Hoffman are highly critical of strategic family therapy, which sees power as central to human relations including family therapy. Hoffman (1990) says:

> According to this second-order cybernetics, living systems were seen not as objects that could be programmed from the outside, but as self-creating, independent entities . . . .

I saw this distinction as a liberation from the models that treated family therapy as purely a matter of behavior change. A first-order view in family therapy would assume that it is possible to influence another person or family by using this or that technique: I program you; I teach you; I instruct you. A second-order view would mean that therapists include themselves as part of what must change; they do not stand outside. This view allows a whole new picture to appear. (p. 5)

Hoffman (1990), moreover, argues the point that power-centered family therapy is an expression of gender bias. She cites psychological research which consistently emphasizes the importance of the male values of independence, autonomy, and control, and less emphasizes feminine values such as relationships and connections.

From the above debate, two prominent themes appear to emerge: One is a view that "power" is a lineal phenomenon; that is, "power" is more accentuated in a lineal relationship, e.g., oppressor-victim, or superior-inferior, than in the context of group, or "circular" relationships. The other is that if the therapist/worker views herself as standing outside the family/group, she views her role to be that of an "objective change agent," who is likely to use manipulative power for influence and change. However, if the therapist/worker sees herself as part of the family/group system and as she becomes part of what must change, the power that is exerted by the worker for control may be significantly diminished by its circumstances alone.

THE ISSUE OF POWER IN SOCIAL WORK WITH GROUPS

Traditionally, social group workers reject the use of controlling and manipulative power in group processes, because the root of social group work is deeply imbedded in a more equalitarian stance than is social casework. Social group work always emphasizes the importance of interdependence of members, equal and full participation by members, and the development of group cohesion. Goals such as "developing a mutual aid system" have been emphasized, and the worker's role as a leader or controller is deemphasized from the onset of the group process. If the worker is seen as a leader in the beginning of the group process, then her leadership is seen as "temporary" or as something of a diminishing role ("she works herself out of a job") and the development of indigenous leadership is always encouraged.

However, a second look at theory among various models in social group work reveals that some models appear to provide more room for the worker's use of manipulative and controlling power than others because of the particular theoretical constructs they rely on.

Furthermore, social group work has traditionally taken a position of "dual perspective" by focusing on individual members as well as the group as a whole. The group is seen as a context for individual change. Many social group work models place more emphasis on change in individual members than in the group as whole. One example is the Organizational model (Glasser & Garvin, 1976) which states:

> The worker focuses on helping each member change either or both his individual behavior or his environment through the group experience. (p. 77)

With this model the worker relies more heavily on social sciences and small group theories for his knowledge base. The model suggests the position of the worker who maintains varying degrees of "objectivity," although he may be functioning as part of the group. In contrast, the Mediation model developed by Bill Schwartz (1976) appears to view the group and the role and function of the worker in a different light. This model appears to have many characteristics similar to those of the second-order family therapist's view of the family. Schwartz (1976) says:

> The worker-client relationship was one in which the client was not an object at all, but a dynamic force with a will and energy of his own . . . . The person retained the ultimate power–using it both consciously and unconsciously–to accept help or reject it, and much of the impetus for change came from the client. Thus, even as the worker strove to "enable" his client, he was himself being enabled by the latter's own motives and energies. (p. 173)

What Schwartz describes here is reciprocity in the relationship between the worker and the client where the power or energies of both parties stimulate and reciprocate each other for growth and development, not a lineal transfer of power from the worker to the client. The worker is part of what must change and a link in an interpersonal web. From this view, such concepts as interdependence, mutuality, or connectedness have greater meaning than the concepts of independence and self-sufficiency.

For a further analysis of the points raised by Schwartz, Falck's new paradigm of the membership perspective appears to provide a useful framework.

In the membership perspective, Falck (1989) argues that the individual and the group should no longer be viewed from the traditional "dual perspective of social work focus," rather they must adopt the membership perspective. He says, "individual and individualism portray a view of human beings that is singular, not social. They do not imply that interaction and exchange are fundaments of human existence" (p. 22). Furthermore, he defines membership in this way: "The term member, like individual, may seem to suggest oneness but, in fact, the term member suggests a minimum of two people, i.e., the smallest group structure" (p. 24). He explained that members are integrated by way of two principles: the principle of constant connectedness and the principle of conditional accessibility.

Thus Falck (1989) defines social work as "the rendering of professional aid in the management of membership" (p. 27). He further comments that "the social worker is a full member of the group and the distinctions between clients and social workers are not to be made on the level of whether or not the social worker is a member, but rather on how the social worker is a member" (p. 27).

THE USE OF SELF

The concept of use of self is by no means new. For instance, both of us attended the University of Pennsylvania, which was known as a Functional School, where the use of self was drilled into our brains by professors like Ruth Smalley and Helen Phillips. But the trouble was that we could not comprehend its meaning, as the concept was stated at a high level of abstraction and vagueness at that time. However, we remember well a phrase such as "the social worker uses the self to release potential power in the client who seeks help from the worker." This statement appears to suggest the roles of the social worker as facilitator, mediator, and stimulator who triggers a release of potential power possessed by the client. The worker would not have been someone who would change the client's behavior by applying technical skills or power of control over the client. However, the problem with the Functional School in those days was that they never specified the kind of stances/skills which were expected of the worker in order to help release potential power in the client. To discover this we will do some explorations now.

It appears to us that how one uses herself in the helping process largely depends on how one views her roles and functions in relation to members or the group as a whole. If one views her role to be that of an expert who treats, for instance, psychopathology, then she is likely to project herself as someone who treats psychopathology of individual persons. Then, in facing a group of people who present a common psychopathology, she is likely to focus her efforts on the correction of this problem in individual members who happened to be in the context of a group. We see many cases of individual treatment rendered by caseworkers who had little training or experience in group work in the context of group treatment. On the other hand, if the worker views herself as someone who attempts to release potential power or energies for action in a group as a whole, she is likely to assume the roles of mediator, facilitator, perspective provider, and stimulator, etc., certainly not the role of therapist or treatment specialist who tries to change a client's behavior as she applies the power of control, manipulation, and other techniques. In order for the worker to assume the role of mediator or facilitator, the worker needs to develop a good deal of self-awareness, and an ability to trust the power of humans for self-growth and change.

Falck (1989) discusses social worker behavior from the membership perspective as follows:

> Ideal social worker behavior, be it in two-member or multiple-member configurations, is never objective or neutral. At its best, however, it is characterized by self-discipline. Social group workers, perhaps more than other social workers, are aware of their own involvement as members among members because of the group structure within which they work. (p. 26)

In the field of family therapy, Terry Real (1990), from the perspective of social constructionism, discusses five therapeutic stances that the therapist may take. Although we should recognize some distinctions between social work with groups and family therapy (Garvin, 1985), some of the stances presented by Real are equally applicable in their essence to social work with groups. It should be noted here that Real uses the term stance rather than technique. Those five therapeutic stances are: (1) *The eliciting stance*. It means that the therapist adopts "an essentially 'one-down' posture," asking for different system members' ideas and theories about "the problem" or "the situation." The therapist resists invitations to rule on one "right" version of reality. (2) *The probing stance*. The therapist offers a new frame, not as an expert revealing truth, but as one member in an evolving dialogue. The goal is different from that of a psychoanalytic interpretation or clarification in which the underlying content is exposed. The therapist claims no special position of expertise. The only strategy is in how he may move himself so as to invite a more interesting conversation. (3) *The contextualizing stance*. This stance is the same as the circular questioning of the Milan Team. Real explains, "The therapist, adopting a contextualizing stance, references a particular move, behavior, or idea in a system out into the interactive field, connecting it to the meta-domain of overall pattern." (p. 264)

Th. And when your brother is truant, who in your family is most upset by that?

Sis. Mother.

Th. And when Mother is most upset by that to whom does she turn?

Sis. Father.

Th. What does Father do?

(4) *The matching stance*. In this stance, the therapist does not do anything in particular with the pattern or tension within the system. She simply mirrors back that which has been shown to her. Real

(1990) considers that the matching stance equates with "empathy" in individual counseling, although she calls it "reflecting" in systems terms. (5) T*he amplifying stance.* In this stance, the therapist chooses a particular idea, affect, theme, or behavioral sequence that is available as a resource within the system and, through her attention to it, evokes more of it. Amplification rests upon the axiom of constructionist therapy: "Often, all one need do to evoke more of any given quality within a system is to attend to it." (p. 267)

CONCLUSION

In this chapter, we have attempted to examine and clarify, from the new paradigmatic positions of second-order family therapy and membership perspective, the concept of power and the worker's use of self in social group work.

These new paradigms have brought new challenge to our conventional thinking about doing social work. They force us to reconsider ways we would use ourselves in relation to the family or group as a whole.

Some of the most salient themes which could be highlighted here are:

1. From the perspective of the new paradigms, the therapist or worker is no longer considered an "expert" outsider who can view the family/group objectively; the fact is that she must consider herself as part of the family/group or "member."

2. As a member, the worker is no longer able to use the power of manipulation or control as a means for change over the system of which she is a part. Rather, she must think how she might use herself with discipline for the benefit of the total system.

3. The worker must think in terms of "mutuality" or "reciprocity" in her relation to members of the family/group and must consider herself in terms of "enabling" others as well as being "enabled" by others.

4. The worker's attention must be focused on "membership," or a group as whole, rather than focusing on individuals in the group.

5. The worker must assume that every person brings to a group something unique, some potential energy for self-growth and ac-

tion. The worker's responsibility is to create conditions where these energies could be unleashed collectively by the members.

REFERENCES

Anderson, H. & Goolishian, H. (1988). Human systems as linguistic systems: Preliminary and evolving ideas about the implications for clinical theory, *Family Process*, 27:4, 371-393.

Bateson, G. (1972). Minimal requirements for a theory of schizophrenia. In G. Bateson, *Steps to an ecology of mind*, New York: Ballantine Books.

Dell, P. (1989). Violence and the systemic view: The problem of power. *Family Process*, 28:1, 1-14.

Falck, H. (1989). The management of membership: Social group work contributions, *Social Work with Groups*, 12:3, 19-32.

Garvin, C. (1985). Family therapy and group work: "Kissing cousins or distant relatives?" In Parnes, M. Ed., *Innovations in social group work: Feedback from practice to theory*, Binghamton, NY: The Haworth Press, 1-15.

Germain, C. (1979). *Social work practice: People and environment, an ecological perspective*, New York: Columbia University Press.

Glasser, P. & Garvin, C. (1976). An organizational model. In Roberts, R. & Northern, H. Eds., *Theories of social work with groups*, New York: Columbia University Press, 75-115.

Griffith, J., Griffith, M., & Slovik, L. (1990). Mind-body problems in family therapy: Contrasting first- and second-order cybernetics approaches, *Family Process*, 29:1, 13-28.

Hoffman, L. (1990). Constructing realities: An art of lenses, *Family Process*, 29:1, 1-12.

May, R. (1972). *Power and innocence, a search for the sources of violence*, New York: W.W. Norton.

Parsons, R. (1991). *Empowerment: Purpose and practice principle in social work*, 14:2, 7-21.

Pernell, R. (1985). Empowerment and social group work, Parnes, M., Ed. *Innovations in social group work: Feedback from practice to theory*, Binghamton, NY: The Haworth Press, p. 117.

Real, T. (1990). The therapeutic use of self in constructionist systemic therapy, *Family Process*, 29:3, 255-272.

Schwartz, W. (1976). Between client and system: The mediating function. In Roberts, R. & Northen, H. Eds., *Theories of social work with groups*, New York: Columbia University Press, 171-197.

Varela, F. (1989). Reflections on the circulation of concepts between a biology of cognition and systemic family therapy, *Family Process*, 28:1, 15-24.

Webster's New World Dictionary (1982). Second college edition, New York: Simon & Schuster.

Chapter 11

Past Practice, Future Prospects: Reminiscence Group Work for the Twenty-First Century

Tom Hopkins

SUMMARY: This chapter is set in the context of reminiscence group work practice in the United Kingdom. Although reminiscence work is utilized in a number of professional fields in Britain–health care, mental health, continuing and "Third Age" education, etc.–the emphasis here is on social work, and specifically within residential and day-care settings. Consequently, older people may also be referred to as "clients" or "service users."

The chapter is specifically concerned with the contribution made by reminiscence group work to the development of a social work practice which seeks to combat discrimination toward older people, and particularly in the form known generically as "ageism."

INTRODUCTION

You have only to begin to lose your memory, if only in bits and pieces, to realise that memory is what makes our lives. Life without memory is no life at all. . . . Our memory is our coherence, our reason, our feeling, even our action. Without it we are nothing . . . ."(Luis Bunuel)

The author gratefully acknowledges the contribution made to the development of a number of themes contained in this chapter by John Harris, Senior Lecturer in Applied Social Studies, University of Warwick, England.

Clearly, human memory is the crucial foundation on which reminiscence works, whether with individuals or groups, depends. Without older people's memories there can be no reminiscence.

There is no question that reminiscence has played an important part in changing human service workers' perceptions of "old age" and of the lives led by older people. By establishing the significance of reminiscence's positive influence on present day physical, mental, and emotional health, workers have helped to counter the negative stereotyping of older people known generically as "ageism."

It is also clear from much of the writing on reminiscence that most workers have tended to operate on the premise that age is the dominant aspect of social identity and social relationships which should shape the content and process of reminiscence. That is to say, it is the fact of being "old" (in the chronological sense) that provides the "raison d'etre" for older people's involvement in reminiscence groups, and which then acts as the mediating dimension of the groups' work.

This chapter argues that such a focus may have obscured the significance of other social dimensions, for example race, class, gender, and sexuality. Moreover, that these will have played an important part in shaping older people's earlier lives; their present recollection of them; and their impact on their current existence. In contrast to the perceived orthodoxy, this paper argues that age cannot be disaggregated from other aspects of social identity and their part in shaping the life experiences which form the focus of work in organized reminiscence groups.

If we assume that reminiscence is only or even primarily about older people's memories as grist to the therapeutic mill, then we are in danger of denying the part that it plays in shaping clients' present day experiences–and vice-versa. How reminiscence group workers, and other group members, react to recollections offered to the group may well influence clients' willingness to share other memories, especially those of a sensitive and/or painful nature. Similarly, how workers and members identify, respond to, and engage with older people's present identities will play a significant part in determining how safe clients feel to further explore their memories in a group-based therapeutic context.

THE BENEFITS OF REMINISCENCE GROUP WORK:
A BRIEF REVIEW

The benefits of reminiscence have been promoted in forms of practice which go beyond the one-to-one work originally proposed by Butler (Butler, 1963). Bromley explains the advantages of reminiscence in group care settings in terms of working with the loss of "a sense of personal identity because of relocation or institutionalisation" (Bromley 1988, 278). Group-based reminiscence, rather than work with individuals, has been the dominant form of practice in British residential and day care settings.

Reminiscence groups are said to offer threefold benefits: to the older person as an individual, to older people collectively, and to the staff who work with older people.

The benefits to older people as individuals have been identified as recreational, psychological, and therapeutic (Norris,1986). Reminiscence has been regarded as stressing the assets of an older person, emphasising individuality and identity, and by so doing, promoting a sense of self-worth (Norris, 1986; Scrutton, 1989).

Older people are also considered to gain benefits from reminiscence through its impact on communication patterns, shared memories leading to more interaction, and of a more intimate nature (Bornat, 1985). The value of encouraging reminiscence by older people as far as staff are concerned is located in the insights provided into older people's formative years, insights which can be used in understanding current problems and uncertainties (Scrutton, 1989; Carter, 1981/2; Martin, 1989; Eleftheriades, 1991).

Another major claim made by reminiscence group workers is that the approach offers a social experience which can be regarded as "anti-ageist." By focusing on positive aspects of old age, they argue, older people are enabled to see themselves–and be seen by others–as still very much socially aware and alive. The act of recalling past events and experiences in a supportive and sympathetic environment is said to increase self-confidence and self-esteem.

As we move through the 1990s and into the twenty-first century, there seems a strong possibility of even more widespread use of organized reminiscence groups, and with a more explicitly anti-ageist focus. Perhaps this is an appropriate point at which to assess the contribution of such groups in that context.

BRITISH REMINISCENCE GROUP WORK AND ANTI-AGEIST PRACTICE

Workers operating within reminiscence groups may have a general belief that they are combating an ageism which is rooted in the marginalization and devaluation of older people by society. Such a sweeping definition of ageism is in itself problematic (Blytheway and Johnson, 1990, 134-135), and this approach to the disaggregation of social divisions, implied by much reminiscence work, needs to be questioned. For example, class as a social division is implicitly at the heart of many organized reminiscence groups.

In Britain, reminiscence groups consist predominantly of working class users of services, most often in institutional or semi-institutional settings. Work in these groups often tends to portray working class older people as "victims" although much is made of their sense of solidarity in times of hardship, and in the face of such adversities as war, disaster, and mass unemployment.

However, by implicitly speaking only to a perceived shared experience of class, this approach runs the risk of ignoring issues of race, gender, and sexual orientation. In other words, membership of one social division can exclude, or virtually exclude, the significance of membership of others.

Such an approach only serves to reinforce a stereotypical view of older people as having led lives in which crucial aspects of their social identities either were of little importance, or have been rendered so by the passage of time. It is as if being old, providing one has respect, is sufficient social identity.

Yet we have increasing evidence that this is not how older people perceive themselves and their social situations. No one can have watched the film *Rosie the Riveter*, in which older American women recalled their experiences of performing heavy industrial work during World War II, without being accutely aware of the powerful impact such involvement had on their social identities, in wartime, postwar, and in later life. Nor could the viewer but notice how strongly these women still felt 40 years later, about the injustice of being displaced from the labor market when men returned from war.

Similarly, the recent elevation of the British homosexual Quentin Crisp to the status of media celebrity in the U.S.A. is worthy of comment in this context. Is it simply the passage of time, and a liberalization of laws and public mores regarding homosexuality in Western society that have made him acceptable where once he was vilified? I would suggest not, and venture that it is in large part because he is now clearly "old" and no longer perceived as the dangerous influence on society which Britain regarded him as 50 years ago. Social workers are familiar with the stereotyping of older heterosexuals as nonsexual beings in later life–by family, friends, and even sometimes by professionals themselves. We need to ask whether the disregarding of older homosexuals' social identities is simply part of the same stereotyping, or a refusal to accept and work with the fact that gays and lesbians remain exactly that in their older age.

As we move toward the next century people will likely bring to their reminiscence groups expectations of a more sensitive response than seems currently in evidence. They will rightly expect workers–and fellows group members–to acknowledge the significance of their racial and ethnic identities; their gender; and their preferred sexuality, as well as their "class." Presently, one obstacle to such an antidiscriminatory practice results, ironically, from the choice of materials offered as a stimulus for reminiscence.

My concern that much contemporary reminiscence work will not provide an adequate foundation for the development of practice in the twenty-first century is reinforced by the present tendency to base reminiscence on "scripts" of a particular kind, utilizing either a set of materials or artefacts to illustrate historical periods as a focus for the group's central themes.

The production of reminiscence packages and kits, based on specific "key" events, disasters, public celebrations, etc., have in recent years become big business for voluntary agencies working in the field of old age. Most residential and day-care settings possess or have access to such materials, and make regular use of them in their reminiscence group work sessions.

The way in which such materials are then used is usually very much determined by the worker. Thus, reminiscence runs the risk of being or becoming a process in which the selection, deployment, and evaluation of materials is very much in the hands of service providers, and very little in the control of service users. This tendency stands in conflict with the alleged change in power relations which reminiscence work is said to bring about (Carter, 1981/2; Scrutton, 1989). This is not to argue that such preselection of materials by workers is necessarily always against the best interests of older people, but rather to raise the possibility of alternative approaches. For example, biographical life histories which are capable of bringing together the impact of a range of social divisions on an older person's life. Where older people are offered more opportunity to shape the content and process of their reminiscing, at least some may choose very different events and activities from those available in a prepackaged form.

As a result of adopting a more reflexive and open approach to the selection of reminiscence content, it is also possible that older people may come to radically different conclusions both about which past experiences they regard as important and the sense they now make of them.

CONCLUSION

Presently, organized reminiscence groups run the risk of implicitly reinforcing ageist attitudes toward older people. Even where respect is shown by workers for older people's life experiences, there is the danger of simply shifting the focus from one stereotypical aspect to another; from a preoccupation with the characteristic of "age" to that of wisdom and the role of "sage."

If reminiscence group work is, in the future, to retain its prominent position in the field of work with older people in forms which contribute to the development of anti-ageist practice, its proponents will have to reconsider their purposes and concerns. Hitherto, a predominantly consensual view of postwar social and economic progress has shaped the content, process, and outcome of reminiscence work. This will soon be replaced by a very different set of political and social realities.

Greater geographical (including international) mobility, changing social and occupational expectations amongst women, increasing numbers of black and other minority group elders are but a few of the features of late twentieth century life that will form part of the individual and collective memories of older people as they reminisce in the 1990s and the twenty-first century.

If reminiscence group work is to contribute to the development of a genuinely radical anti-ageist practice, it needs to begin from the ambiguities, tensions, and contradictions of older people's earlier lives and allow the possibility of them reflecting on their experiences and interpreting them in new ways.

Group workers may find that, offered such opportunities, older people's views of their experiences and of past events in general may not add up to a coherent and conflict-free whole, but rather remain fragmented, ambiguous, and troublesome for them and their carers. If such a shift of approach by group workers is to occur, it calls for them to more clearly identify their theoretical and ideological allegiances.

This, in turn, will call for a review of models and approaches currently deployed in the service of reminiscence group work. It is unlikely that a "treatment" or "therapeutic" orientation will suffice as the conceptual and theoretical foundation for reminiscence group work in the next century.

REFERENCES

Blytheway, B., and Johnson, J. (1990). "On defining ageism," in *Critical Social Policy,* pp. 127-139.

Bornat, J. (1985). "Reminiscence: The state of the art," in *New Age,* Summer, p. 14-15.

Bromley, D. B. (1988). *Human Ageing. An Introduction to Gerontology,* Penguin.

Bunuel, L. (Original source unknown).

Butler, R. N. (1963). "The Life Review: An Interpretation of Reminiscence in the Aged," in *Psychiatry,* 26, pp. 65-76.

Carter, J. (1981/2). "Long ago but not quite forgotten," in *New Age,* Winter, pp. 28-30.

Eleftheriades, S. (1991). "Remember, remember . . . ," in *Social Work Today,* 25 April.

Martin, J. M. (1989). "Expanding reminiscence therapy," in *British Journal of Occupational Therapy,* 52, 11, 435-436.

Norris, A. D. (1986). *Reminiscence with Elderly People,* Winslow.

Scrutton, S. (1989). *Counselling Older People. A Creative Response to Ageing,* Edward Arnold.

Chapter 12

Social Group Work in Hong Kong: Future Challenges for the 1990s

Bing-Kong Choy

INTRODUCTION

The signing of the Sino-British Agreement on the future of Hong Kong in 1984 led Hong Kong into a transitional period through to July 1997, when the sovereignty of the territory would be resumed by China. Hong Kong shall become a Special Administrative Region enjoying a high degree of autonomy. Our present form of capitalist system with executive, legislative, and independent judicial power will be preserved for fifty years from 1997 onward. In a nutshell, this is the widely publicized concept of "one country, two systems." Before 1997, the British administration has to deliver the power into the hands of Hong Kong people through a process of political democratization. This signifies that Hong Kong has been undergoing deep changes, not only in the realm of politics but in other social fabrics of the society. The task of "Hong Kong people rule Hong Kong" is unprecedented since Hong Kong people have concentrated largely in economic activities, leaving the government administration and policy decisions to a vast and efficient Weberian type of bureaucracy for the past 100 years.

The implementation of a representative government since 1982 has aroused and stimulated much concern and greater participation in the affairs of Hong Kong. However, the June 4th incident in

China in 1989 had resulted in uncertainty about future and a confidence question in the future government of Hong Kong. Emigration becomes a common phenomenon in Hong Kong. People are subtly categorizing one another as stayers or goers. For those who stay behind, they will have to face the pains of separating from their family members and friends as well as the stress of living in a society driven to achieve and an obsession with material wealth.

Social group work, as any other institutionalized activity in society, is not practiced in a vacuum but is significantly influenced by its contexts. As Hong Kong is being reshaped in its political, social, and economic dimensions during this transitional period, it is important to identify what issues will confront us as social group workers so that we can make decisions and take actions that are proactive rather than just reactive to the changing context. Examining the future of social group work in the 1990s will impel me to move backward in time to search for a better take-off point for moving ahead in the future. It is this connection between the roots of social group work and future directed growth that will be examined.

In this paper, I shall first review the changes of group work practice in Hong Kong for the past decades. These changes in practice are actually reactions to the changes in the contexts of practice. My purpose is to point out that our group work practice has been largely influenced by the external environment which consists mainly of the economy and social system. The second part of this paper is to anticipate and speculate what is to come before 1997 and what challenges will be posed to group workers in Hong Kong.

AN HISTORICAL SKETCH

An analysis of the group work practice and other social work interventions in Hong Kong will obviously link up with the political and socio-economical conditions of Hong Kong. Several observations can be made about the characteristics of social welfare in Hong Kong. First, although the level of resources allocated to social welfare represents about 6 percent of the total government budget, the financing of our welfare budget depends totally on the performance of our economy. Second, our government has financed almost all the welfare services from the general revenue and no attempt has been made to establish any contributory or cost-sharing schemes. Third, there is an absence of a coherent and comprehensive policy about the development of welfare services in Hong Kong. Fourth, the government still owns the view that social welfare is a charitable, non-productive burden borne on the back of the "normal," productive institutions of the economy. Social welfare services were assigned a secondary place as they should never interfere in the market. The quantity and scope of welfare provisions were decided by the bureaucracy, based on the available resources of each year.

Similar to the origins of group work in Western countries, group work was first started in Hong Kong by the boys' clubs, Ys, and scouting during the early 1950s. Early group work concerns centered around acculturation of refugees to the urban scene, skills training, education, and recreation. Basically group work at that time mainly consisted of the efforts of missionaries and charitable organizations.

The role of government in social welfare became significant in the 1960s when it published its first policy paper on social welfare. However, the development plans were shattered by the riots in 1966 and 1967. The government realized that the youth problem was becoming more serious while the family system in Hong Kong was rapidly disintegrating. A great number of young people were involved in the two riots and their antisocial behavior shocked the government. Consequently, all sorts of programs were launched to help youngsters spend their excess energy. Recreational activities for the youth were given top priority and groups were organized in community and youth centers. This has anchored the role of groups in children and youth services which then became the mainstream in youth services. Group work was considered both as a method and a service for the youth population and it developed a close bond with recreation and informal education.

Theoretical advances in the 1960s also set the direction for group practice in Hong Kong. The social goals model postulated by Papell and Rothman was widely adopted by community centers in their organization of volunteer training and social service groups while the remedial model was used in working with young offenders at the correctional institutions and hostels. The practice of group work was largely confined only to youth services and community organizations and considered as secondary to the one-to-one case interviews in family service agencies.

The context of practice changed in the mid-1970s when the juvenile crime rate drastically increased. Other than organizing remedial groups for the juvenile offenders, preventive and developmental groups were organized in various settings such as the schools and playgrounds where the youngsters were located. Coupled with other interventions, group work served the function of control in combating juvenile delinquency. On the other hand, groups were run by family counseling as well as elderly service centers which manifested the choice of group work as one of the major intervention strategies.

Economic growth in Hong Kong began to regress in the 1980s which directly affected the rendering of social welfare services. Pressures of expediency and cost effectiveness of group work emerged. Social problems became more complicated as less resources were allocated by the government. Mutual aid groups would seem to be the appropriate solution to cope with the limitations of manpower and resources.

To recapitulate, certain comments on the group work practice in Hong Kong can be made:

1. With the proliferation of models and approaches to working with groups, there is a confusion about what social group work is and what it should be. In Hong Kong, social workers are involved in many different types of groups ranging from recreation and skills training to sensitivity training groups. It seems that anyone can work with groups, and did. The problem lies in the lack of a firm identity of social group work which tries to work with a wide variety of client groups but finds its usefulness being challenged.
2. The values of group work in Hong Kong changed as the perception of social welfare developed. At first, group work was seen as a type of service rather than a method. It then represented a method of working effectively with a wide range of

client groups and symbolizes a new approach to demands which overburden social work teams. Currently, its use may reflect a search for an economic use of resources or an antidote to doubts about the effectiveness of casework. Its attractiveness may lie in the conviction that people can be understood and helped only when they are considered alongside the systems and networks in which they function.

3. Despite the variable positions of group work in social work, many social workers would still consider group work as another demanding responsibility placed on top of an already substantial workload and undertaken without supervision. It requires, therefore, a high degree of commitment and enthusiasm for any practitioner to offer to do it and to establish a continuity of experience which allows the development of skills and knowledge as group workers.

4. Groups nowadays, are primarily organized in the areas of skills learning, recreation, and socialization. Members of such groups normally expect a structured, organized experience through the use of programs. Very often, the programs become the ends replacing the original group purposes and reduce the expressions of emotions. There is also the risk of overcontrolling through programs by the group workers who feel that they have limited training in group work.

5. Groups in Hong Kong are frequently too short to achieve their objectives or to consolidate the progress made. Indeed, the length of many groups is often determined prior to the recruitment of members. Consequently, the nature of many groups will be task-oriented, behavior changing, or acquisition of skills.

6. Many social work practitioners still feel ill-equipped for group work, lack confidence, and are concerned about the level of their skills and capabilities. Agencies' support and the co-operation of colleagues are difficult to obtain in view of their feelings about group work in their setting: envy, indifference, scepticism, about its utility, and concern about increasing caseloads. Besides, there has always been an eagerness from the group workers to acquire techniques that proved useful in group process while neglecting the purposes of the group and characteristics of group members.

THE FUTURE CHALLENGES TO GROUP WORK

Predicting tomorrow in the realm of human services is hazardous, especially under the current unprecedented socioeconomic changes, heralded by the democratization of political structures of Hong Kong. Besides, since group workers in Hong Kong have never reached a full agreement about group work methodology, we cannot expect consensus about the future of group work. In fact, I hope my predictions still stimulate debate and development of ideas about what the future direction of group work in Hong Kong should be.

REVIVAL OF GROUP WORK FUNCTION

While it is true that group workers are involved in many different kinds of groups, they have not neglected some of the best traditions of social work: democratic procedures, basic respect for human dignity, a concern with the social environment, and attention to the welfare of those in need. In the beginnings of group work practice, the group is the means to such ends as participatory democracy, social action, and social change. These traditions are evident in the new roles that group workers are assuming today in facing the unpredictable future of Hong Kong society. If the Hong Kong people are going to rule Hong Kong, then participation from all walks of life, particularly those from the low stratum, are vital. The challenge is to reinforce rather than withdraw from the social change potentials that are created whenever people join together. We have to reintroduce an understanding of the importance of community participation and strengthened communities into the purposes and methodologies of groups with which we work. Group workers in the 1990s will promote more social action by means of client activation, group confrontation, and advocacy. Henry Maier (1970) suggested "the focus is upon vitalizing the client's own competence in effectively entering into the change efforts of his changing society . . . . The stress is upon the client's competence in effecting change rather than upon social change per se." Coyle (1947) further emphasized that group work provides an "experience in democratic participation," is a "schooling in democracy," and is a mode of social action "in the creating of a better society by orderly and democratic methods" of social change. This indicates that the element of social change has to be reworked and reworded in the future of group work practice of Hong Kong.

ENABLING CLIENTS' CAPABILITIES

The major characteristic of the social welfare system in Hong Kong is to provide minimal assistance to those who are not able to help themselves. The government has a perennial belief that social development must be an appendage of economic growth and a traditional view that social services are acts of benevolence of the government or charitable organizations. Therefore it is unlikely that we will ever have all the resources we would like for social services. As in China's own so-called social welfare system, work performance and contribution to the common good are considered as determinants of welfare entitlement (Jones, 1990). There is no reason to suppose the same ethic will not be expected to prevail among the Chinese people in Hong Kong after 1997. We can expect that any improvements in social welfare will have to be 'earned,' collectively by continued economic high performance; individually by personal and family effort. The challenge is for the group workers to use diminishing resources to maintain group services. This implies that group workers have to develop the mutual care and concern potentials of the client groups. According to Schwartz (1961), the group "is an enterprise in mutual aid, an alliance of individuals who need each other, in varying degrees, to work on certain common problems." It is a helping system in which the clients need each other, to create not one but many helping relationships, which is a vital ingredient of the group process and constitutes a common need over and above the specific tasks for which the group was formed. Thus the challenge is to legitimate the value of working with mutual help groups and to sharpen practitioners' skill in working with such groups.

COPING WITH RAPID CHANGES

Moving forward to a renewed concern about the health of individuals throughout their life cycle and in their interaction with the shifting social milieu of Hong Kong, we see a special place for social group work practice. Hong Kong people have been living under great stress due to crowding, pollution, and an atmosphere of competition since childhood. With the advent of the 1997 takeover, almost every Hong Kong resident is besieged by the stress of confidence crisis about the future of Hong Kong. Other problems that we have to encounter include inflation, an increasing violent crime rate, and a sunset government that is not capable of melding the shaken social fabrics of Hong Kong. This distress handicaps people in their work, their personal relationships, and their family life. In various ways they are experiencing an inability to cope with life's problems. The challenge to group work is to strengthen or create ways of working with groups that are responsive to these issues. One of the crucial ways is to help group members to overcome feelings of powerlessness and futility in facing the 1997 question. Furthermore, the use of groups for treatment purposes will continue to grow, for the individual casualties of a fast-paced, changing society are heavy and the group treatment milieu has great utility.

FOSTERING INDIVIDUAL GROWTH

Living in Hong Kong in the 1990s is very similar to what Toffler describes in his book *Future Shock*. Toffler (1970) identified three characteristics of changes society faces today: transience, novelty, and diversity. He postulated that the effects of acceleration of change will force an individual to "live faster," and people of the future will live in "a condition in which the duration of relationship is cut short." In interpersonal relationships, duration and depth become increasingly limited. There is also a search for a sense of belonging, a kind of social connection that confers some sense of identity. Accompanying this is a bewildering diversity of values with people becoming more narcissistic. Under the rapid pace of social change, the "normal" process of growth and development becomes highly problematic. Life's developmental crisis periods intensify their demands on individuals for successful resolution. The achievement of a stable identity, a consistent set of core values, a sense of self-actualizing direction, and a capacity for intimacy that reaches beneath the superficial level of transient relationships may require social services beyond the institutional arrangements of family, church, and school. The challenge to group work is to provide experience over time that helps stabilize the personality, giving it depth and meaning; to help individuals together to cope with the forces of change. Tropp (1969) upheld that "group work, is, in effect, the primary social work practice in a position to meet people at the point of average functioning, and the primary one with the structure and method to undertake the task." To this can be added Clara Kaiser's (1959) words, "social group work has its major contribution to make in focusing on building ego strengths of individuals and on the social health of groups."

CONCLUSION

Gazing into my crystal ball has revealed that group work will continue to flourish in this decade as an important part in social work. The expected drastic changes in various aspects of Hong Kong society before 1997 will bring group workers close attention to participatory democracy, social action, and social change along with the more individualized goals of the group work method. "Programming" and "recreational activities" will become less important and workers are more concerned about the group processes and interaction than the achievement of tasks. The synthesis of the past with the emerging new trends toward assessment of outcomes and effectiveness of services will widen the horizon of social group work. Henry Maier (1970) suggests that a group has to bring together a wide spectrum of age ranges and persons of different segments of life because living with diversity, coping with the predictable, and finding a personal integrity amidst many others are the challenges of today. Indeed, these are the same challenges that group workers will meet in Hong Kong between now and 1997.

REFERENCES

Chow, W. S. "Welfare Development in Hong Kong–The Politics of Social Change" in Y.C. Jao, ed., *Hong Kong and 1997.* Centre of Asian Studies, University of Hong Kong, 1985.

_____ "A Review of Social Policies in Hong Kong" in Alex Kwan, ed., *Hong Kong Society*. Writers' & Publishers, Cooperative 1986.

Coyle, G. L. *Group Experience and Democratic Values*. New York: The Woman's Press, 1947.

Garvin, C. "The Changing Contexts of Social Group Work Practice: Challenge and Opportunity" in *Social Work with Groups*, Vol. 7(10), Spring 1984.

Jones, C. *Promoting Prosperity: The Hong Kong Way of Social Policy*. The Chinese University Press, 1990.

Kaiser, C. *The Social Group Work Method in Social Work Education*. New York: Council on Social Work Education, 1959.

Maier, H. *A Sidewards Look at Change*. Seattle: University of Washington, 1970.

Schwartz, W. "The Social Worker in the Group" in *New Perspectives on Services to Groups: Theory, Organization, and Practice*. New York: National Association of Social Workers, 1961.

Toffler, A. *Future Shock*. New York. Random House, 1970.

Tropp, E. (1980). "A Humanistic View of Social Group Work: Worker and Member on a Common Human Level" in Alissi, A. ed. Perspectives on Social Group Work Practice: A Book of Readings, The Free Press.

Chapter 13

The Action Component of Group Work Practice: Empowering the Client

Kenneth E. Reid

Action in the form of doing, achieving, performing, and experiencing has, over the past seven decades, been an essential component of the group work method. Likewise, action is fundamental in social work's historical commitment to empower people to make life-giving choices and gain control over their environment.

In spite of its historical prominence, the social worker who leads groups is often faced with the very practical issue of finding viable ways of assisting group members to act in their own behalf. Too often, passive absorption and ponderous introspection in the search for self-knowledge are substituted for action. Members gain valuable insight but demonstrate limited long-term behavioral change. Rather than becoming empowered, they experience paralyzing inertia, apathy, dullness, and deadness–feeling as if they are drowning in a whirlpool of words.

It is through a combination of self-knowledge and action in group work that members are empowered to act upon their world in a constructive, reasonable, appropriate, and life-enhancing manner. This chapter examines the use of action in small groups from a

Appreciation is expressed to Dr. Marion Wijnberg, Western Michigan University, for assistance on an early draft of this chapter.

person-in-situation perspective with the goal of clarifying its function vis-à-vis the helping process.

ACTION AND GROUP WORK TRADITION

The action component in group work is long-standing. It was evident in the early social movements that fostered group work including progressive education, settlement, recreation, adult education, and the playground movement. Action was an essential part of the pioneer leisure-time and youth serving agencies such as the scouts and the Ys who used small groups as a means of socialization and character building. The significance of action was visible in the seminal writings of Mary Follett, Jacob Riis, Eduard Lindeman, Grace Coyle, John Dewey, and Alfred Sheffield who provided a theory base for group work. The value of action was reported in the records of the early youth leaders and recreation workers who creatively used programming activities such as dance, music, crafts, and games as a way of effectively helping hard-to-reach adults and children. The action component was accentuated in the efforts of the social reformers and their fight for social justice, and the empowering of immigrants, minorities, and the unemployed to actively participate in the democratic process.

In the early years the action component differentiated group work from the more dominant social casework. For example, group work emphasized member versus client; doing *with* versus doing *for*; doing versus talking about doing: activity and others as primary agents in the helping process versus the worker alone as the primary agent; personal and social development and social contribution as legitimate professional foci versus a remedial and rehabilitative focus; health and strength versus sickness and breakdown (Pernell, 1986).

In and through the small group, members are provided the opportunity to make and act on choices in their effort to accomplish the group's purpose and their own individual goals. The small group is an ideal modality for raising consciousness, engaging in problem solving, mutual aid, self-help, changing institutions, and experiencing one's own effectiveness in influencing others.

BALANCING TALK AND ACTION

As psychology and psychiatry have increasingly influenced group work, insight and self-knowledge achieved through the use of interpretation and introspection have taken on greater importance. Similarly, there has been a reduction in the attention given acting and doing. Maluccio (1974), observing a similar phenomenon in casework suggests the limited attention given to action is due to the importance placed on feelings, the primacy of clinical dialogue, and the lack of a theoretical framework capable of providing an adequate rationale for the use of action. According to conventional wisdom, healing the psychological roots of a problem is a prerequisite to changing the client's attitude toward life. This has, according to Perlman (1975), been based on the "questionable assumptions" that if a person feels better it will inevitably follow that the person will act better. And that if the person understands better, he or she will do better. From this change in attitude, it is assumed, the person will develop more effective patterns of living which over time will solve his or her psychological difficulties.

Insight derived from the past is not, by itself, an effective instrument for growth (London, 1971; Perlman, 1975). Too often the insight and the interpretations that produce the insights serve only to provide the person greater self-understanding but result in limited change. According to Douds, Berenson, Carkhuff, and Pierce (1967):

> Insight may, seemingly, reduce confusion by subsuming the conceptualizations he has about himself in a neater package, allowing him the illusory belief of being "on the top of his problems"–he can now explain his anxiousness on high level terms. Victimized by a wishful need for a magic solution, he accumulates insights based on his reactions to different people and situations, hoping for THE ULTIMATE INSIGHT which will be an answer to everything. (p. 172)

Paralyzed to act, the client remains dependent and passive, noticeably lacking action and direction in his or her existence.

Corrective change does not occur just because the client places the problem before the worker and/or group, and vents disturbing feelings. Nor does it happen because the client and the worker agree that certain actions ought to be taken. Corrective change requires a preplay in preparatory ways, an exercise of the ego capacities for perception, anticipation, imagination, judgement, self-observation, awareness of the other, choice, and other ego processes insofar as they are present and accessible. In sum, corrective change requires a balance of both self-knowledge and action (Perlman, 1975).

ACTION AND MASTERY

A feeling of mastery and control over one's internal reaction and environment is a significant part of the growth process. We see this in an infant who begins to manipulate objects; in the five year old who learns to read; in the adolescent who obtains a driver's license; in the adult who builds a cabinet or cooks a special meal.

To cope with a problem is to intentionally undertake some new or different form of action in addressing the problem. Such action may be the modification of thought or feeling that occurs through a fresh perception or perspective of an experience. Or, action may be in the form of taking a small step within the orbit of the problem toward altering one's own behavior, the behavior of another, or of a condition.

The capacity to influence the forces which affect an individual's life space for his or her own benefit leads to a beginning sense of competence and control. The development of mastery alleviates feelings of helplessness by boosting the persons's ability to cope. Conversely, rejection, despair, and depression can result when the person perceives him or her self as a helpless and powerless victim of forces beyond his or her control. There is the sense of feeling trapped and helpless to act constructively in his or her own behalf. Having transferred the locus of evaluation and sense of direction to external forces, the person feels ruled by significant others, fate, society, rituals, obsessions, and "luck."

In his research on learned helplessness, Seligman (1975) reports a significant correlation between reactive depression and the person's belief that their actions will have little or no impact on the outcome of a situation. Often acquired early in life, there is the expectation that the individual will not be able to control outcomes, and that their sense of helplessness is proof that they are basically inadequate in every aspect of their life.

Argyris (1964) observes that in helping individuals move toward adult maturity, certain basic tasks have to be accomplished. These include:

1. Change from a passive to a more active state.
2. Change from a state of dependency on others to relative independence.
3. Change from behaving in a few ways to acting in many ways.
4. Change in interests, with erratic, shallow, and temporary interests giving way to mature, strong, and enduring interests.
5. Change from a present-oriented time perspective to a perspective encompassing past, present, and future.
6. Change from solely follower or inferior relationships with others to relationships as equal or superior.
7. Change from lack of a clear sense of self to a clearer sense of self and control of self, thus to more confidence in controlling one's fate.

These developmental tasks, according to Argyris, are accomplished slowly over a lifetime, and progress is often uneven and sometimes erratic. Progress in accomplishing these tasks can be impeded by a number of factors including the person's competence, problems of confidence, and lack of motivation.

BEYOND HELPLESSNESS AND POWERLESSNESS

Individuals view themselves as having power or as being helpless and powerless in terms of the economic system, the political system, religious and educational system, and the legal and justice system (Cox, 1988; Hartman, 1987; Parsons, 1991; Solomon, 1976). At a more immediate level is their asymmetrical power relationship with family members, peers, and fellow group members. As clients experience a lack of control in relation to their environment, that experience is internalized. Reenforced over time, this sense of impotency has the potential of creating the dynamic of debilitation and self-blame. Seeing no feasible options, they may think of themselves as unable to change their lives. They feel increasingly overwhelmed with the obstacles and helpless to improve their situation.

Often our clients are in pain, feeling themselves victimized, and experiencing no choices or freedom of action. According to Bandler and Grinder (1975), it is not that their world or choices are limited but, instead, that the clients block themselves from seeing the options and possibilities that are open to them. Thus, a significant part of the change process becomes that of expanding the client's models of the world. Ideally, through the group experience, participants increase the accuracy of their perceptions, and enlarge their resources–personal, communal, and organizational, enabling them to gain greater control over their environment and to attain their aspirations.

RELUCTANCE TO CHANGE

Risk-taking, like change of any kind, is a step into the unfamiliar and the unknown. Even through group members make a decision to do something different, they often become stuck and unable to move. Faced with the unfamiliar, they hesitate on the brink with mouth dry and heart pumping in the face of the unknown. Repeatedly, they sabotage their long-term good, acting as if they were adversaries to the very life, joy, and vitality they desperately crave.

Others share the propensity to act in ways that are self-defeating rather than ways that are life-expanding. They recognize the cost of their behaviors but are unable to alter their actions. Like a sailboat that is becalmed in the water, they drift aimlessly without direction, hoping for some external force to rescue them. Egan (1990) likens this reluctance to act to the law of inertia in physics that states a body at rest tends to stay at rest unless something happens to move it along. For some, the source of inertia is immobilizing fear. Others lack competence, confidence, or willpower.

Some clients have assumed a passive mode in various life situations that call for action, and choose to do nothing. They neither respond to problems nor to options. Feeling victimized, they overadapt, or uncritically accept the situation so as not to rock the boat. There are those that engage in random or agitated behavior or become incapacitated or violent, either shutting down or blowing up (Schiff, 1975).

There may be disabling self-talk that can reenforce the feeling of helplessness and powerlessness. Subconsciously (and sometimes consciously) group members repeat to themselves deprecatory messages such as:

- "I'm inadequate."
- "I can't cope."
- "Everyone is better than I am."
- "It's no use, life is stacked against me."
- "Nothing good ever happens to me."

Such self-defeating internal conversations, when allowed to go unchallenged, establish a mind-set and prevent the person from going beyond the immediate "what is" and thinking in terms of "what could be."

Effective group work requires participants to make a basic plan of action, commit themselves to it, and use the tools offered by the group process to explore ways of carrying out the plan. Too often there is vagueness in establishing a specific direction, making it easy to put off doing something about the problem. The participant may be reluctant to set goals or objectives fearing they will never be accomplished, and result in a greater sense of failure.

ACTION IN AND THROUGH THE GROUP

Members become empowered in and through the group experience. It is the worker's responsibility to build an optimum group experience so as to enable individuals to exert the power they have to make changes and obtain needed resources. This raises several therapeutic as well as pragmatic questions. First, how do we intervene within the group in such a way that the members realistically increase their perception of themselves as having power over the forces that control their lives? Second, how do we prepare clients to take appropriate risks and begin to effectively act upon the decisions they have made? Third, how do we encourage members to act upon their world in a reasonable, appropriate manner that strengthens them inwardly and enables them externally?

Action by members, in and through the group, can be separated into five interlocking and overlapping bipolar categories. First, action can be *external* or *internal*; that is inside the person's head or overt and seen by others. Second, action can take place *during* a group session or *outside* the group. Third, there are *personal* actions related primarily to a member, or *political* actions which clients take individually or collectively to influence existing realities. Fourth, actions can be a *formal* part of the group structure, or *informal*, occurring in a serendipitous manner not part of the overall plan.

Exactly how we utilize or encourage action in the member's best interest will depend upon a number of factors including the purpose of the group, the group's objectives, and the social-emotional capacity of the members (Reid, 1991).

External and Internal Action

External Actions. External actions are those overt behaviors that can be observed by others, either in the past or present. Some examples of overt behavior in groups include:

- A member who consistently arrives late.
- A man who blames others for his problems.
- A woman who is immobilized with fear and does not speak.
- An adolescent who calls another member names.

In these examples, the member learned the behavior through past experience. None of the individuals are bad, crazy, or sick but rather are making the best choices from those of which they are aware (Bandler and Grinder, 1975). As the person comes to new moments of living he or she utilizes these old behaviors as a way of coping with their environment.

During a group session, members or the group-as-a-whole can be challenged to examine external behavior, particularly if the behavior is found to be self-defeating or harmful to others. For example, the worker may confront the group–gently or strongly to mobilize resources so as to take another step toward deeper self-recognition or constructive action.

A common target of confrontation is the illusion of work in which verbalizations and action are in reality a form of resistance.

Individual members or the group-as-a-whole, while appearing to grapple with important issues, in fact avoid significant work on the problem. Such a challenge by the worker may precipitate a crisis that disturbs, temporarily, the member's personal and social equilibrium. Ideally, the confrontation by the worker and/or other members leads to greater self-confrontation both inside and outside the group.

The individual will look to the others in the group for approval, support, and reinforcement. Opinions and attitudes of fellow members as well as the worker will influence the person's perception of his or her own success and failure in trying out new behaviors.

Internal Actions. Internal actions, on the other hand, are those processes that go on inside the person's head and include such activities as thinking, daydreaming, rehearsing behaviors, imagining, remembering, planning, deciding, and perseverating on an idea. According to Ellis (1973) and others (McMullin, 1986; Wodarski and Harris, 1987), the objective of counseling is to assist the client to exercise control over his or her internal action, e.g., being controlled by old tapes or negative self-talk. Some examples are getting a woman member to challenge her particular interpretation of reality, or, getting an adolescent to examine his distortions in thinking, having drawn a conclusion when evidence is lacking or contrary to the conclusion.

Clients who have been traumatized generally need assistance in identifying themselves as survivors rather than helpless victims. This is especially true for children who have been sexually or emotionally exploited. Their perception of the experience–often based on reality, is that there was nothing they or their parents could do to stop the event. According to James (1989), there is a striking similarity between children who have assumed a helpless victim role and adults who become bogged down in purging emotions related to childhood and who do not move on in their lives. Such individuals can learn that there is life after victimization through sharing with others who have successfully integrated similar experiences. Evolving from victim to survivor can also occur through learning and rehearsing the move from powerlessness to effectiveness by role playing and direct practice.

The benefit of sharing past suffering is not so much a cathartic emptying of personal pain, but the act of bearing witness to one's suffering, being believed, listened to, and understood without judgement (Freud, 1988). All are affirming experiences as is the sharing of sexual secrets followed by the implicit or explicit reassurance from the worker and/or fellow group members.

Action Inside and Action Outside the Group

Action Inside the Group. Talking and doing within the group can be a force for producing action. Action inside the group occurs when a member tries out new, potentially positive ways of initiating behavior with other members and the worker. It occurs when the member tries out new, potentially positive ways of responding to other members and the worker. It occurs when individuals in the group reveal significant information they have previously kept to themselves.

The group offers a unique setting for both diagnosis and intervention. Because of the here-and-now nature of group work, interpersonal and intrapersonal problems are exhibited in vivo in the worker's presence, rather than retrospectively recited hours or days later. The worker is provided the opportunity to objectively observe the group member's behavior, his/her perception of the situation, plus the reaction of others.

Action Outside the Group. During group sessions, members address problems and issues they are facing with significant others, e.g., family members, employers, etc., and then utilize new behaviors and insights in dealing with these people. In most problem situations, the alternatives are infinite; but, when under stress or facing a crisis, an individual's view of the multitude of options available is restricted. Once there is a clear definition of the problem, a useful technique is to invite the member as well as the group as a whole, to brainstorm and identify as many options as possible. Examining, analyzing, and listing alternatives to consider should be as collaborative an activity as possible.

Personal Actions and Political Actions

Personal Actions. Personal actions enhance the self-image and competence of an individual. It occurs by group members nurturing and being nurtured, by being givers as well as takers. Personal action occurs as members make decisions about their own lives. Referring to therapeutic self-help groups for women in abusive relationships, Hartman (1987) writes that the women gradually transfer their ability to be self-responsible within the group to their life outside the meetings. Their locus of control begins to change with members becoming proactive rather than reactive. They discover they have choices about their sense of identity, self-esteem, sexuality, communication style, and the way they spend their time. They learn that they cannot control others or all aspects of their own lives but can feel new power in making the choices open to them.

Encouragement and group support are an essential ingredient as group members begin to experience their own inner resources and the power to choose for themselves, and take charge of their lives. The social atmosphere of equality, which characterizes group work, exerts one of the most effective and therapeutic influences on each of its members.

Political Actions. Political or collective actions have to do with clients gaining leverage and achieving greater control over their environment (Cox, 1988). During this period of diminishing public resources, it is particularly important for the social worker to recognize there is not an "either/or" situation between collective and individual empowerment (Staples, 1990). Both are necessary in enhancing the well-being of individuals who comprise the group. Examples include the individual or group negotiating problematic situations and changing existing social structures.

Sometimes the target of political action is the same private and public social service agencies the client depends on for assistance and resources. Because of the disparity of power, clients may feel reluctant to request needed services. It becomes the worker's task to skillfully assist them to become empowered both individually and collectively. Hasenfeld (1987) suggests a number of possible worker strategies for empowering clients to harness organizational resources in their own behalf. These strategies include providing clients with greater information about the agency and its resources; training clients to assert and claim their legitimate rights in the agency; increase the clients knowledge and expertise in handling their needs; and linking clients to a supportive social network that can lend them resources so as to reduce their dependency upon the agency. Finally, the worker can empower clients by teaching them when threats or disruptions may be effective tactics in obtaining needed resources.

Formal and Informal Action

Formal Action. Formal actions include skill training, assertiveness training, role-playing, and behavioral rehearsal in which troublesome situations for group members are recreated. Other group members and the leader participate by coaching and playing the roles of significant others in the member's life. Another formal activity is the systematic use of homework assignments. These assignments involve the client in the collection of basic information about his or her behavior in relationship to the environment. In addition, the client is encouraged to follow certain suggestions and bring back news on the effects of the assignment.

Informal Actions. Informal actions are those activities that members do on their own or with little or no guidance from the worker. Through interaction within the group, individuals develop problem-solving skills, support, and increased alternatives. They expand their horizons, gain a firmer, more authentic sense of self, take new risks, and lead an examined rather than an unexamined life. With this as a base, members sometimes meet socially or to accomplish a task that may or may not be directly related to the group. This is illustrated in a self-help group for women who had been sexually abused. The members decided to participate as a collective in a "take back the night" march, by walking together, as a way of showing their support.

The major difference between formal and informal actions is that formal actions tend to be planned and part of the group's structure while informal actions are casual, spontaneous, and of a serendipitous nature.

PRACTICE PRINCIPLES

The group member achieving growth-producing insight and knowledge is not enough. This insight and knowledge needs to be integrated into the person's life, inside and outside the group. The following practice principles empower the individual and the group-as-a-whole to action.

An action orientation needs to prevail throughout the group's development. From initial interview to termination, it is important that members and worker share in the belief that intentions and talk only count if they are translated into action. As practitioners, we must continuously ask ourselves, in what way can the member apply the knowledge and skills learned in the group in his or her own behalf? An action orientation means group members holding each other accountable to the expectation of each going beyond their comfort zone and making life-enhancing choices oriented toward truth, dignity, integrity, honesty, and courage.

The worker should view him or herself as a facilitator, collaborator, and partner with the group members. Consistent with the principle is the importance of the worker doing *with* rather than doing *to* or *for* the group. If the members are to be helped to extricate themselves from a stressful situation and to gain a functional personal-social balance that is satisfying and enduring, they must be active rather than passive participants in the group.

Action tasks to be accomplished will vary from member to member. For some individuals it is necessary that the action steps be small and well practiced beforehand. For others, action steps can be much larger and occur spontaneously. The greater the client's emotional disturbance, the smaller the action-tasks should be and the greater the necessity for rehearsal within the group.

Members need to set specific and realistic goals for themselves. An action-orientation requires that clients identify what they want from the group, and articulate relevant short and long range goals for themselves. In the early stages of the group, goals may be general. As the group progresses, these goals need to be made more specific. As part of setting goals, alternative actions and probable outcomes also need to be examined.

Action outcomes, whether successful or unsuccessful, need to be evaluated in the group. Whatever action-task the member or group as a whole assumes, it is necessary that the results–positive or negative–be discussed as to what worked and what did not work. Often, for a variety of reasons, the group or member is unable to carry out a planned task. Here again the dynamics along with future plans need to be addressed in the group.

The worker needs to be willing to challenge and confront members to examine their internal and external actions. Such challenges are a responsible unmasking of the discrepancies, distortions, and smokescreens the person uses to hide both from self-understanding and from constructive behavioral change. The purpose is to reduce the ambiguity and incongruities in the client's experiencing and communication.

Feelings of anger need to be honored, affirmed, and mobilized. When there is an atmosphere of trust, support, and safety, reenforced by the ground rule of no physical abuse, participants feel free to express resentment, rage, and anger toward the leader and fellow members. It is not enough for these feelings to be addressed in the abstract, intellectual, or in a once-removed manner. Instead, participants are encouraged to trust the feelings and, when appropriate, verbalize them directly to the person. Conflicts between members are to be worked through by assertive communication and problem-solving skills. Discomfort of anger diminishes as members discover they will not be rejected or abandoned when they are angry.

BY WAY OF CONCLUSION

This chapter's intent is to underscore and illuminate the significance of an action orientation in group work. Action has long been a part of group work tradition, and is an essential ingredient in the change process. Personality structure and strength are affected by the person's ability to make complex decisions and to act effectively to achieve his or her goals. Many individuals feel helpless and powerless to act or prevent action, and it is the function of social work to empower people to take effective action–individually or collectively, in their own behalf. In and through the group there are multiple, overlapping, and bipolar potential forms of action. These include internal and external action, personal and political action, formal and informal action, and action inside and outside the group. Finally, by encouraging positive action, the worker assists members and the group as a whole to move beyond apathy, inertia, dullness, and deadness to greater self-definition and wholeness.

REFERENCES

Argyris, C. (1964). *Integrating the individual and the organization.* New York: Wiley.

Bandler, R. & Grinder, J. (1975). *The structure of magic I: A book about language and therapy.* Palo Alto, CA: Science and Behavior Books.

Cox, E. O. (1988). Empowerment of the low income elderly through group work. *Social Work with Groups, 11* (4), 111-125.

Douds, J., Berenson, B. G., Carkhuff, R. R. and Pierce, R. In search of an honest experience: Confrontation in counseling and life. In R. R. Carkhuff and B. G. Berenson (Eds.), *Beyond Counseling and Therapy,* (170-179). New York: Holt, Rinehart, and Winston.

Egan, G. (1990). *The skilled helper: A systematic approach to effective helping* (4th.ed.). Pacific Grove CA: Brooks/Cole.

Ellis, A. (1973). Rational-emotive group therapy. In G. Gazda (Ed.), *Group Therapy and Counseling.* Springfield, Illinois: Charles C. Thomas.

Freud, S. (1988). *My three mothers and other passions.* New York: New York University Press.

Hartman, S. (1987). Therapeutic self-help group: A process of empowerment for women in abusive relationships. In C. Brody (Ed.), *Women's Therapy Groups: Paradigms of Feminist Treatment,* (67-81). New York: Springer Publishing.

Hasenfeld, Y. (1987). Power in social work practice. *Social Service Review, 61* (3), 469-483.

James, B. (1989). *Treating traumatized children: New insights and creative interventions.* Lexington, MA: Lexington Books.

London, P. (1971). *Behavior control.* New York: Harper and Row.

Maluccio, A. (1974). Action as a tool in casework practice. *Social Casework, 55* (1), 30-35.

McMullin, R. (1986). *Handbook of cognitive therapy techniques.* New York: W. W. Norton.

Parsons, R. J. (1991). Empowerment: Purpose and practice principle in social work. *Social Work with Groups, 14* (2), 7-21.

Perlman, H. H. (1975). In quest of coping. *Social Casework, 56* (4), 213-225.

Pernell, R. (1983). Old themes for a new world. In P. Glasser and N. Mayadas (Eds.), *Group Workers at Work: Theory and Practice in the '80s* (pp. 11-21). Totowa, NJ: Rowman & Littlefield.

Reid, K. E. (1991). *Social work practice with groups: A clinical perspective.* Pacific Grove, CA: Brooks/Cole.

Schiff, J. L. (1975). *Cathexis reader: Transactional analysis treatment of psychosis.* New York: Harper and Row.

Seligman, M. (1975). *Helplessness.* San Francisco: Freeman & Co.

Solomon, B. (1976). *Black empowerment: Social work in oppressed communities.* New York: Columbia University Press.

Staples, L. H. (1990). Powerful ideas about empowerment. *Administration in Social Work, 14* (2), 29-42.

Wilson, G., and Ryland, G. (1949). *Social group work practice.* Cambridge, MA: Riverside Press.

Wodarski, J., and Harris, P. (1987). Adolescent suicide: A review of influences and the means of prevention. *Social Work, 32,* 477-483.

Chapter 14

Treating the Chronically Ill in an Outpatient Hospital Setting: Does Group Work Work?

Zoë Levitt
Elizabeth I. Lewis

SUMMARY. Recent advancements in medical technology have afforded individuals suffering from chronic illness with the opportunity of a prolonged lifespan. While this phenomenon brings with it a feeling of success and accomplishment, it can also lead to a whole host of individual, family, and societal problems such as decreased self-esteem, altered family dynamics, and underemployment to name a few. The literature cites social group work as one method of helping individuals and families cope with these problems.

Within the past two years, the authors of this chapter have been involved in a multidisciplinary support group geared toward individuals receiving Home Peritoneal Dialysis, and their families. It is the intent of this chapter to describe and analyze the nature and effectiveness of this group, using the results of qualitative, evaluative research completed for this purpose. Specifically, the authors seek to determine whether group work is a viable intervention for a chronically ill out-patient population that is required to maintain ongoing dependence on the hospital. Recommendations for the most appropriate group work model will also be suggested.

THE GROUP

The group was initiated in 1988 by five members of the Home Peritoneal Dialysis team, including two social workers, two training nurses, and a clinical nurse specialist. The objectives of the group were to provide emotional support and education, to enhance level of functioning, and to create a forum where individuals could share ideas and strategies for coping. Originally, the intention was that the group would take on a self-help model. This did not prove realistic however, and staff maintained the roles of coordinating the meetings and acting as group facilitators. This significant observation will be discussed further in the paper.

Patients and family were informed about the group by means of a letter. A sign was also posted in the clinic area. For a period of approximately four months, staff telephoned the patients who were scheduled for clinic that week to remind them about the group and to "invite" them to attend.

The format of the group was open-ended and intended for both patients and family members. Meetings were held twice monthly for one hour after clinic in a room adjacent to the home dialysis training area. As the meetings began at noon and many of the patients had been in clinic since early morning, a light lunch was provided.

The atmosphere of the group was intentionally kept informal. People came when they could and sometimes left early to keep other appointments. One nurse and one social worker attended each meeting on a rotating basis. The numbers of patients/family members who attended varied from meeting to meeting. Generally, there were five to six participants present each session.

The Evaluation

After the group had been running for approximately 16 months, an evaluation was completed to determine the group's effectiveness and to obtain more general information on the patient population. A questionnaire was developed as the tool for evaluation. Completion of the questionnaire was voluntary and all information was collected anonymously.

A social work student distributed the questionnaires to all patients and family members at the clinic, regardless of whether they had attended a group meeting before (non-attendees were asked to comment on why they had not come to the group). The student was available to assist with completion of the questionnaires if needed. While patients/family members were encouraged to complete the questionnaire during the clinic visit, some chose to take it home and return it to the office at a later time. It is important to note that distribution, assistance in completion and collection of the questionnaires were all handled in a consistent manner.

The Results

The Participants

Ninety-one individuals out of a population of 116 completed the questionnaire. In some instances, the patient and a family member filled out the questionnaire together, while at other times it was done separately or only by the patient. Forty-six women and 45 men ranging in age from 17 to 82 participated in the evaluation. The majority of the population (79 percent) were over the age of 40 and 44 percent were over 60. The age range of those who attended the group was 24 to 82 years.

Most respondents were married (65 percent) and most had been on Home Peritoneal Dialysis for three years or less (83 percent). Seventy-six percent were not employed (this included 34 percent who considered themselves unable to work, 30 percent who indicated they were retired, and 12 percent who stated they were unemployed). Of those employed, 22 percent worked full-time and 2 percent worked part-time.

Attendance

Fifty-four percent of respondents had attended at least one group meeting. Of these, the majority had attended two or more sessions. The most frequently expressed reasons for limited or non-attendance were: "transportation problems"; "group not useful"; "must return to work"; "limited English"; and "not wanting to spend an extra hour at clinic." Other reasons included: feeling "too tired or unwell"; "not being comfortable in groups"; and needing to "return to family at home." One person did not attend because family did not want to stay.

Likes/Dislikes About the Group

Answers to the question regarding what people liked about the group were categorized into four areas: discussion and information sharing (21 responses); support (12 responses); "everything" (4 responses); and socializing (2 responses). Some examples of comments included: "information about dialysis, swimming, and traveling"; "talk about common problems and experiences"; "support, not alone"; and "get others' perspective." Twenty-eight percent of respondents reported that coming to the group had made a difference to them.

Seven people listed dislikes. These were expressed by comments such as: "not enough information conveyed"; "depressing–a group of sick people makes me sick"; and "depends on who is there– sometimes one person can take over and does not let others talk."

Concerns Expressed by People on Dialysis

To assist in determining if the group was addressing people's problems/concerns regarding dialysis, respondents were asked to list these under various headings. The most frequently mentioned category of concerns was physical problems (46 responses). Specifically, these included feeling tired; nausea; change in appearance; decrease in appetite; numbness in legs; and limited mobility. Emotional concerns such as depression; anger; frustration; sadness; being fed up; mood swings; and "poor me" feelings were identified by 23 respondents.

Lifestyle was the next most frequently cited category. Twenty people expressed concerns relating to decreased travel; decreased sports activities; and feelings of restriction ("cannot go anywhere"). Occupational concerns noted by 15 respondents included working fewer hours; feeling too sick to work; and being unable to find work which accomodated dialysis. Sexual concerns were reported by 14 respondents. Specifically they noted impotence; decreased desire; decrease in feeling "sexy"; and "difficulty in finding a boyfriend." Eleven respondents stated that they had financial concerns relating to unemployment, working fewer hours, and the cost of medications. No spiritual concerns were identified by our population. Most people felt their spirituality was unaffected, while three people reported feeling stronger and happier.

Interest in Increased Group Involvement

Only 7 percent of respondents indicated an interest in becoming involved in the planning and/or running of the group and only two individuals gave their names. Forty-four percent stated they were *not* interested in increasing their involvement.

Suggestions for Future Group Sessions

The questionnaire offered 23 suggested topics for future meetings. Responses included requests for discussion around: dialysis related issues such as peritonitis, traveling, activity/exercise (69 responses), kidney disease, transplants, and the Kidney Foundation (48 responses); and psychosocial issues such as sexuality, depression, family stress, and stress management (37 responses). Legal and financial issues were mentioned as potential topics, although not very frequently (6 and 4 responses respectively).

DISCUSSION

In an attempt to assess the overall effectiveness of our group, it is important to first consider several factors individually.

Target Population

We chose to open the group to all patients *and* family members. There was a wide range of ages (24-82) among group participants and thus they represented many different stages in the family life cycle. Further to this, there were both new and experienced dialysis patients and their families in attendance. As a result, the target population was quite diverse and, interestingly enough, this did not appear to impede the group process.

The issue of including both patients and family members in the same group is a significant one. Our rationale for doing this was based on two observations. First, prior to the beginning of the group, staff had noted spontaneous groupings taking place among patients and family members in the clinic waiting area. Clearly, patients and family members alike were seeking support and they appeared able to give/receive it in the company of each other. Second, on a more practical note, family members often accompanied the patients to clinic and thus it was not realistic to expect them to wait idly the additional hour while the group was in process. A discussion around the benefits and limitations of including family members and patients in the same group will take place later in the chapter. Regarding our group's experience, we found that the inclusion of both was not problematic.

Another interesting aspect of our group population was the presence of both new and experienced dialysis patients in the same meeting. We observed two different phenomena that were, according to our results, associated with this. First, as was noted above, group participants identified a sense of satisfaction with being able to gain support and knowledge from each other. Persons new to dialysis learned from the experience of the veteran participants, while the veteran group obtained fresh perspectives from the newer people. This phenomenon is also noted and described as beneficial by other authors (Buchanan, 1978; Toseland & Siporin, 1986).

In addition to this experience of mutual aid however, there was also the dual experience of hope and despair in meeting with persons who had lived with the illness for many years. While it is true that individuals may have been encouraged by seeing for themselves how others had successfully coped, they may also have felt dread in seeing those who were suffering further physical deterioration or difficulty in adjusting to the illness. This was reflected in our results by one respondent who commented that the group was depressing because "a group of sick people makes me sick."

Format

A major question for the group facilitators was that of format. Should the group be open-ended or closed? What would be the frequency of meetings? When dealing with a chronically ill out-patient population, one must always consider the overall health and well-being of patients. In view of our population, we felt that the most realistic option was to couple the time of the group with the clinic so that interested persons would be able to attend both in only one trip to the hospital. The key issues here are practical and emotional. From a practical standpoint, many patients were either frail elderly or simply unwell and thus not able to make additional visits to the hospital. In some instances, patients were working or attending school and could not spend any more time away from these activities.

From an emotional standpoint, it is true that there are often many negative feelings associated with the hospital that make it difficult for patients to spend what they consider "extra" time there. This idea is an important one and will be elaborated on later in the chapter.

In choosing an open-ended format and in keeping meetings bi-monthly, we allowed patients and family members the freedom to attend the group as often or as infrequently as they wanted. In turn, we believe this facilitated an atmosphere which encouraged participation because it gave participants a sense of control, something which they are robbed of in the disease process. Contrary to this perceived benefit, our open-ended format gave little opportunity for members to form relationships and develop a sense of cohesiveness. This was illustrated in our results by the poor response (7 percent) to the question on increased group involvement. Without the sense of commitment that comes from feelings of belonging, could we expect that persons would take responsibility in the planning and running of the group? Clearly, the answer is no. Another factor which may have effected the outcome of this question is that of physical well-being. As mentioned above, fatigue is a common experience among dialysis patients. It may also be that individuals were simply too tired to allow for further participation.

Attendance

We felt it was positive that of those attending the group, the majority came two or more times. Several authors (Buchanan, 1978; Sorenson, 1972; and Toseland et al., 1990) have suggested that persons with chronic illnesses tend to seclude themselves and that this social isolation promotes the belief that they are alone in their experiences. In view of this, it is reasonable to assert that group meetings would help an individual understand that they are *not* alone. Specifically, it would allow that person to experience mutual support, solidarity, and acceptance (Buchanan, 1978; Abrams, 1980).

Was our group effective? Twenty-eight percent of respondents reported that coming to the group had made a difference to them. In addition to this, our results showed that we were able to address our objectives of providing emotional support and education, enhancing functioning, and creating an opportunity for sharing in the group. Thus overall, the authors believe the group was a success. A key question is left unanswered however. Why did it appear that the group did not grow in popularity over time? If individuals found the group beneficial, why did the staff have to continue to actively recruit group members?

We must remember that we are working with a hospital outpatient population who present with unique characteristics. Inpatients, by definition, are suffering from an acute medical problem. Often accompanying this is emotional distress. By virtue of their hospitalization, they are immersed in their illness and cannot readily deny their situation. For these reasons the inpatient population is generally more accessible, physically and emotionally, to groupwork interventions. In contrast, outpatients have usually already overcome the emotional crisis and have reestablished their coping mechanisms, whether adaptive and/or maladaptive. Outpatients are no longer living in the hospital and, for the reasons outlined below, are more difficult to engage.

There are definite barriers to providing groups for outpatients in the hospital setting. However, we prefer to substitute the term "challenges" for barriers as it better reflects our belief that they can be overcome. Unfortunately, there is a dearth of literature regarding these challenges. Thus, based on relevant readings and the analysis of our own support group, we have identified the following three challenges.

Reminder of Loss

To outpatients and families, the hospital serves as a visual reminder of loss of health and the accompanying stresses/emotional battles. Whenever a patient must return to the hospital for a routine yet mandatory clinic appointment, this individual will likely experience a sense of emotional discomfort. Of course, the intensity and severity of this will vary from person to person.

For the majority of the chronically ill there is no "escape" from the hospital, and for many, from their illness. As a result, dialysis patients or, in fact, any chronically ill person may find it difficult to attend a group in the hospital setting. Here the challenge is for staff to find non-threatening ways to overcome this and encourage individuals to join the group. We identified telephone calls as one effective means. Patients felt supported and personally touched that staff would actually take the time to call them about the group.

Practical Considerations

As discussed earlier, chronically ill outpatients must often rely on relatives to transport them to and from the hospital. Group facilitators must somehow find a way to accommodate for this. One option is to open the group to both patients and family. There are advantages and disadvantages to this however. When they meet together, patients and family members are given the opportunity to understand the others' experience of the illness more objectively. Whether they are observing their *own* relative interact in the group process, possibly expressing feelings and concerns, or whether they are hearing the perspective of an unrelated group member, the point is that the individual will benefit from the experience of the illness in a different context.

On the other hand, it is also true that both patients and family members may feel reluctant to discuss certain concerns in the presence of their loved one for fear that it would upset or anger them. While it might be considered acceptable for an individual to talk about his/her *own* feelings in a group setting, it may feel too exposing/threatening to have a discussion about family relationships and problems in the presence of strangers.

Emotional Functioning

The literature cites endless research concerning emotional functioning of those persons afflicted with chronic illness. Generally, these individuals feel that needing emotional help is considered a sign of weakness. Despite this finding, the literature also states that these individuals do, in fact, undergo a difficult period of emotional adjustment with regard to the illness experience (Buchanan, 1978; Abrams, 1980; and Sorenson, 1972). Thus, the skill in offering a group for these patients in which they *can* feel free to experience support from other group members is a significant challenge for any staff member. This undoubtedly proved to be the case with our group. We learned that if we promoted the group as a "support" group, inevitably patients would comment that they were managing "well" and did not feel the need for it. Nevertheless, when patients did attend the group, the need to express feelings and concerns was prevalent.

Recommendations

What type of group model, then, is the most effective and therapeutic? For the chronically ill out-patient population, we believe that psychotherapeutic or self-help groups may not, in all likelihood, lend themselves as effective modalities. Instead, we strongly suggest that a psychoeducational group will serve the complex needs of this population. The literature cites that this groupwork format has many non-threatening, yet therapeutic benefits. The educational component meets the overriding need that the chronically ill have for concrete information. Buchanan (1978) writes that "Knowledge implies security and its acquisition reduces the anxiety that arises from the often exaggerated fears of the unknown future. Even the most emotionally stable patients and their families want to know more about their disease" (p. 430). This argument is also substantiated by other researchers (Lubell, 1976; Hartings et al., 1976), and has been confirmed in our findings.

The educational component then, serves as a non-threatening way for members to ultimately begin to allow themselves to feel emotionally supported and to be able to acknowledge this. The ability to learn from others and, similarly, to give to others can be of utmost therapeutic value. This is particularly true for the chronically ill who often experience a shattering of the self and a decreased feeling of control (Toseland & Siporin, 1986; Northen, 1983; and Sorenson, 1972).

Given the inherent challenges in providing a group to the chronically ill, outpatient population, it is our opinion that this group should be psychoeducational, open-ended and one that includes family members. The responsibility of the group leaders is to promote as much group participation, learning, and support as possible. Although this might appear to be quite an eclectic approach to the group process, our experience has demonstrated that this format is of therapeutic value.

REFERENCES

Abrams, Louise A., "A Study of Group Therapy with Dialysis Patients: The Integration of Education into the Therapeutic Group Process," *Dialysis and Transplantation,* 9(3), March 1980, pp. 213-217.

Buchanan, Denton C., "Group Therapy for Chronic Physically Ill Patients," *Psychosomatics,* 19(7), July 1978, pp. 425-431.

Buchanan, Denton C., "Group Therapy for Kidney Transplant Patients," *International Journal of Psychiatry in Medicine,* 6(4), 1975, pp. 523-531.

Hartings, M. F., Pavlou, M. M., and Davis, F. A., "Group Counselling of M. S. Patients in a Program of Comprehensive Care," *Journal of Chronic Disease,* 29, 1976, pp. 65-73.

Lubell, Derryl, "Groupwork with Patients on Peritoneal Dialysis," *Health and Social Work,* 1(3), August 1976, pp. 159-175.

Northen, Helen, "Social Work Groups in Health Settings: Promises and Problems," *Social Work in Health Care,* 8(3), Spring 1983, pp. 457-476.

Sorenson, Ewald T., "Group Therapy in a Community Hospital Dialysis Unit," *Journal of the American Medical Association,* 221(8), August 1972, pp. 899-901.

Toseland, Ronald T., and Siporin, Max, "When to Recommend Group Treatment: A Review of the Clinical and the Research Literature," *International Journal of Group Psychotherapy,* 36(2), April 1986, pp. 172-201.

Toseland, Roland W., et al., "Comparative Effectiveness of Individual and Group Interventions to Support Family Caregivers," *Social Work,* May 1990, pp. 209-216.

Chapter 15

What Are We Teaching as Group Work?
A Content Analysis
of Undergraduate and Graduate Syllabi

Elizabeth Lewis

At the Thirteenth Symposium of AASWG's in Akron, Ohio, a syllabus exchange for course content in teaching social group work was introduced. The following material is based on a content analysis of syllabi received from 14 baccalaureate and 10 graduate programs in the U.S., Canada, Britain, Hong Kong, and Israel. A total of 50 separate course outlines were received. This is a self-selected sample. In addition, a brief review of titles of papers accepted for the symposium was done to identify foci of interest and practice. The presentation is in three parts:

(1) Topical areas and frequent resources in both undergraduate and graduate programs: variations/topics in course content, and teaching options;
(2) Suggestions from respondents for ways of improving teaching of group work practice in class and field;
(3) Increasing the availability of instruction for both practice and supervision of practice through:
    (a) continued pressure on CSWE to strengthen and improve standards and the compliance with standards for curriculum content on small group theory and social group work practice;

(b) development of non-university resources for practitioners and supervisors, following the patterns set by
family therapists.

WHY SHOULD WE BE AGGRESSIVE IN PROMOTING
EDUCATION FOR THE PRACTICE
OF SOCIAL GROUP WORK?

There are practical reasons for improving education for social
group work practice, beyond our belief in the *centrality of group in
life*. A recent study done by the Survey Research laboratory of
Virginia Commonwealth University (1991) commissioned by the
American Board of Examiners through the National Institute for
Clinical Social Work Advancement (NICSWA) has identified some
startling facts. NICSWA has a membership of 20,000 Board Certified Diplomates, a grouping that might be considered the cream of
clinical practitioners in social work. Of the sample of 5,000 sur-
veyed, and districted by census tracts, 38% lead groups as a method
of service; 49% of graduates post-1981, utilize a group method. Of
the total, only 26% indicated any training in social work practice
with groups. When family practitioners realized that MSW education did not prepare them for practice with families they began to
develop Family Therapy Institutes and provide certification for
family therapists as specialized practitioners. Schools of social
work, primarily graduate programs, began to incorporate units,
courses, and finally concentrations on family practice and family
therapy into the regular curriculum. The demonstrated interest and
need did more to change graduate curricula than any pressure from
CSWE With this frequency of practice with groups greater preparation and formal training is needed.

At one time, the practice of social group work was recognized as
a specialized form of social work, requiring special training, even
four semesters of both theory and practice. While we have refined
the basic social work knowledge required of all social workers, the
generalist foundation, now taught in both baccalaureate and first
year graduate education, it is still possible to organize the specialized content by the nature of the social entity to be helped, i.e.,

families, groups, and organizations, as well as by the problem or age of population: health care, addictions, youth, aged, women, etc.

While we do not have a representative sample of course outlines from schools and programs (self-selected respondents), it is clear that some programs continue to offer education for targeted social entities, namely groups. Some programs, primarily at the graduate level, make it possible for students to enroll in as many as four courses, some required, others elective. At the baccalaureate level because of the nature of requirements, and the usually smaller size of faculty, it is less possible to have the flexibility of both required and specialty courses in group work, although some programs have been able to do that.

I conclude that whether we agree that social work should be as heavily clinical (therapeutic, remedial) as it seems to be, there is a clear need for systematized and formal impartation of social group work knowledge, and further, there is a ready market for nonuniversity education. Perhaps we should recall our own roots of development–practice needs and agency initiated education. The AASWG and its member chapters have, potentially, a great opportunity to improve social work practice with groups through the development of regional institutes, continuing education courses, offerings that meet the licensing requirements of the several states, and ultimately impacting upon the formal course offerings of schools and programs of social work.

WHAT ARE WE TEACHING AS GROUP WORK?

A Bit of History

In 1983-84, I conducted a survey of all undergraduate and graduate programs in the United States and Canada through the encouragement of AASWG. At that time the findings were discouraging for it seemed that what was taught about practice with groups drew from everywhere but social work, that our own literature had been abandoned in favor of alternative and allied disciplines. Graduate programs generally abandoned the "entity" frame (individual, family, group, and organization) for organizing curriculum in favor of problem areas, particularly health and mental health, although family and child welfare held its own. (There was federal training money available). Baccalaureate programs labored to incorporate all the required content for the professional foundation along with the institutional requirements for basic liberal education, a CSWE requirement as well. Many undergraduate programs utilized a "systems" framework for the HBSE content, the theory base, but practice courses were heavily oriented to work with individuals. Individual, family, and group were to be covered in one or two courses, organizations and organizing in one course. As we know, there is a rich variety of content for work with individuals, and that coupled with student interest usually weighted the courses. Group theory and practice with groups barely hung in. It was clear that in many programs the instructor made little distinction between small group theory and social work practice with groups. The base for understanding the complex dynamics of interpersonal interactions between and among members/participants was very weak. The systems frame provided the base for appreciating the inter-connections of persons, group, agency, and wider community/society, a holistic perspective that early practitioners knew from their neighborhood agency orientations.

What appears to be happening is a refinement and amplification of the connectedness of entities, an operationalization of systems thinking. This seems to have made it possible to turn greater attention to basic theory about families and groups, (we never lost the emphasis on person/behavior theory), and thus to somewhat more appreciation that there are specialized methodologies required to assist both families and groups.

Now to move beyond the historical review to current course content:

In spite of our critiquing, and wishing for greater recognition of the value of special education for social group work practice, group work is alive and well, at least in some circles! Although baccalaureate programs generally teach a generalist model, *some* content on group theory is included in the HBSE sequence. The systems frame emphasizes the interactive effects of relationships between and among persons, families, small groups, neighborhoods, organizations, and the wider society, a positive base for more specific content-group theory. Practice courses usually include work with groups, not in depth, and non-conceptually, often not very technically. However, our undergraduate syllabi offer a good basic coverage of practice concepts. (We could work on the development of an "ideal" basic course.)

The graduate syllabi reflect the opportunity for more inclusion, greater depth of conceptual knowledge, and specialized technique. There is a range of content, and also of organizing principles. Courses might be classified in the following categories:

- basic: these explore theoretical perspectives about groups, usage, and accepted group processes: most include phase or stage theory;
- advanced: these explore and help students to experience a range of techniques for practice;
- differential uses: these explore the various facets of practice with diverse populations, particularizing the knowledge and skill needed to serve such populations;
- non-deliberative: (program) these, much more frequently identified in this review than in the 1984 survey, include both conceptual content and practical experience with a range of media, modified for various populations and problems;
- therapeutic: these focus on the processes of formation, grouping, and ways for worker and members to deal with the common circumstances, or perhaps, common emotional responses to traumas of many kinds. There is increased awareness that the group medium is the method of preference; self-help, mutual aid groups outside of social work have brought this recognition to clinical practitioners. (Note my earlier remarks about the number of clinical practitioners utilizing the group mode.)
- task-oriented: these examine the characteristics, required competencies, needed by members/participants and the level of development of group as instrument for accomplishing external tasks: staff groups and teams, community groups, planning, and organizing groups are all examined. This is an encouraging trend, and courses which focus on these kinds of purposes are more frequent than in 1984.

There appears to be a great range, scope, and versatility in the content and mode of organizing the group work courses. Many are able to capture student interest by incorporating current problems and populations at risk in the course focus: bereaved children, battered wives, and gay men, as examples. Some weave the population and problems with particular methodologies/ technologies: battered wives/issues of power and dominance, gender discrimination as a focusing theme for practice and goal; or, adolescents, drugs, and identity, where the group medium may be the major interventive mode.

While case-oriented workers may be more tuned into the affective component, the group worker can deal with behavior, action, interactions visible to all members, shared by many, and with present emotional responses of participants. This public, social group data is often overlooked by unskilled practitioners, with a consequent lack of movement within the group.

Literature and Resources

The annual symposia of the AASWG, the proceedings, and the journal *Social Work with Groups* have produced a remarkably versatile, broad range set of resources for practitioners and academics. There is a marked change from 1984, when much of the literature was drawn from other than social work practice with groups. While the "classics" of the 1960s continue to be used, many of the more recent books written in the 1980s now appear on the reading lists and the syllabi: Alissi, Garvin, Gitterman, Ephross and Vassil, Toseland and Rivas, Shulman, and Brown. It is less clear just what texts are utilized for basic small group theory. This content may be embedded in other than the social work courses, particularly at the undergraduate level where students are required to develop their liberal arts base in sociology, anthropology, and social psychology. Some of the more recent authors have woven the small group theory into the texts on practice, but there still appears to be a tendency to confuse/use some non-social work texts in practice courses.

Teaching Methodologies

There is diversity in teaching methodology. Numbers of syllabi indicate use of the class as an analogue for small group practice.

There are problems with this. Yes, there are parallels with educational groups with predetermined content. And this practice may sensitize students to the interactional processes generated within class groups. There are no automatic parallels with groups in practice, and some of the techniques used to develop student sensitivity and "self-consciousness" may not be appropriate to groups in practice. Focus on feelings tends to minimize group action and emphasize the talk medium. Clearly, the intent is to enhance experiential learning, an important goal especially where students do not have a concurrent group experience in their field assignment.

Several syllabi call for course projects, especially where students do not have the field experience. The student is expected to think through in a hypothetical situation such things as group formation and composition, goal setting, and decision making, without actually doing these things with a real group.

The traditional use of case (group) records and of video continues. Taping of vignettes for review is available with proper equipment. A major complaint is the lack of real life group work practice experience, or coordination of class and field, and thus the opportunity to teach from experience.

Students are expected to provide a record of service or to note critical incidents for review and analysis, an option available only to those with direct group experience. A number of syllabi have useful exercises or require a research project. Some of the graduate course outlines offer student options in assignments, thus encouraging student creativity in learning.

Thirteenth Symposium Content Analysis/Themes

It seemed pertinent to make a brief review of the topics and papers we are offering in this symposium as a way to note where our attention is focused.

Group Types: (1) family-like, (2) support/self-help, (3) residential, (4) task-oriented, (5) bereavement, (6) children, (7) elderly, (8) foster care, (9) stroke, (10) working couples, (11) substance abusers, (12) males.

Theory bases/issues: Theory is not often identified, issues of authority and intimacy, gender-related, feminist theory, psychological theory.

History/Philosophy. Methods: (1) use of self, (2) clinical/therapeutic processes, (3) research instruments, (4) effectiveness, (5) group work/case work principles, (6) planning for, (7) multi-family groups, (8) socio-education, (9) empowerment processes.

Populations/Problems. Sexuality, abuse, homeless women of color, residential, medical personnel, workers, consumer boards, intercultural, care givers, and dementia/schizophrenia.

Standards for Group Work Education. (1) faculty development, (2) field education, (3) processes of supervision.

As can be seen by this quick review, the range and diversity of our interests covers most of the current populations at risk, and issues of personal discomfort. It does not reach to the social issues of poverty, racism, and sexism except as these are manifested in groups organized to assist with personal coping.

Notes and Suggestions for Improving the Teaching and Learning of Practice

We asked our respondents to give us their ideas for improving teaching and practice of group work. These are the responses.

1. Include small group theory in the HBSE courses: i.e., reintroduce and teach a full content on small groups.
2. Develop field experiences with groups for all students; include the requirement in the field syllabus, and work with field agencies to introduce the group method of service where appropriate.
3. Introduce/provide field instructor training for development of and supervision of group work practice.
4. Continue to support the monitoring of the CSWE standard on inclusion of social group work content.
5. Continue the symposia.

SOME SUGGESTIONS FOR INCREASING THE AVAILABILITY OF INSTRUCTION FOR BOTH PRACTICE AND SUPERVISION– A ROLE FOR THE ASSOCIATION

It is clear that the Association for the Advancement of Social Work with Groups has provided a reference group and professional support for practitioners and educators. It has enhanced the writing about and expansion of ideas and written resources for both teaching and practice. We are now in a position to move beyond "self-help" to address some of the institutional weaknesses hampering the full development and availability of this central practice method. The following are suggested for our consideration:

(1) Examine the route of family therapists, i.e., begin to develop short or long-term institutes under chapter auspices, or utilize a panel from AASWG for programs done with chapter members, or in cooperation with university continuing education and/or state level NASW.
(2) Explore becoming a "provider" in those states requiring continuing education credits for recertification for licensure; this can be a moneymaker for local chapters and can showcase local practitioners as well as outside panel members.
(3) Utilize/influence university continuing education offerings by providing the course instructor, syllabus, and participants.
(4) Build relationships with agencies providing a group approach to particular at-risk populations, i.e., being able to support and strengthen the social group work method. Know some basic principles of member ownership, democratic process, development of *group,* and inclusion of *structural* or *contextual* goals.

In short, we need not expect schools and programs to carry the load. We need to initiate teaching-learning opportunities from practitioners for practitioners. If you are a faculty member, consider how you, with the chapter, may utilize special topics, conferences, mini-symposia as means of delivering content, and making money for further efforts. You should utilize your membership in the AASWG for support, back-up, and consultation. No one will do it for us. We must be pro-active in our own behalf.

REFERENCES

National Institute for Clinical Social Work Advancement, *Board Certified Diplomates: Contituent Profile Survey,* prepared for American Board of Examiners in Clinical Social Work, with assistance from Survey Research Laboratory, Virginia Commonwealth University, Richmond, VA 1991. Judith Bradford, PhD, and Edna Roth, PhD, principal investigators.

Syllabi: Undergraduate Programs:

#1. *BAR ILAN*
   a. SW46035: 2nd year, 3rd year

#2. *BEN GURION*
   a. #14411151,14411161

#3. *BLOOMSBURG, PA*
   a. SW45.450 syllabus & bib.
   b. Research Project

#4. *COVENTRY POLYTECHNICAL (Britain)*
   a. syllabus

#5. *DELAWARE STATE*
   a. SW39.411

#6. *HONG KONG*
   a. syllabus #1-Choy
   b. syllabus #2-Pearson (MSW)

#7. *NORTH EASTERN ILLINOIS*
   a. SWK360 syllabus & bib.

#8. *NORTH CAROLINA STATE*
   a. SWK98M syllabus & readings

#9. *RADFORD UNIVERSITY*
   a. SW423 syllabus, exercises, bib.

#10. *SAN FRANCISCO STATE*
   a. SW401 syllabus & bib.
   b. SW832 syllabus & bib.
   c. SW833 seminar

#11. *UNIVERSITY WEST FLORIDA*
   a. SOW3322 syllabus & bib.

#12. *WILLIAM WOODS COLLEGE*
   a. SW3143 syllabus & bib.

#13. *UNIVERSITY WISCONSIN-EAU CLAIRE*
   a. SW471 syllabus & bib.

#14. *WRIGHT STATE-OHIO*
   a. SW482 syllabus & bib.

Syllabi: Graduate Programs:

#15. *BOSTON UNIVERSITY*
   a. SSW760 Levinsky syllabus & bib.
   b. SSW760 Duffy syllabus & bib.
   c. SSW760 Walker syllabus & bib.
   d. SWW760 Shulman syllabus & bib.
   e. GW 762 Shulman advanced syllabus & bib.
   f. GW 760 Garland syllabus & bib.
   g. Miscellaneous outlines
   h. GW 761 Task Oriented syllabus & bib.

#16. *CONNECTICUT*
   a. 704-331 GW I syllabus & bib.
      outline F/ group proposal
   b. 704-332 GW II syllabus & bib.
      group analysis, assignments
   c. 704-333 SGW III syllabus
   d. 708-340 Group Process syllabus & bib.
   e. xxx Use of Program & bib.

#17. *DENVER*
   a. SOWK 4350 syllabus & bib.

#18. *INDIANA*
   a. SW 312 (BSW) syllabus & bib.
   b. SW 634 (MSW) syllabus & bib.
      outline, group prospectus

#19. *LOUISIANA STATE*
   a. SW5102 Practice I syllabus & bib.
   b. SW5326 Practice II task groups syllabus & bib.
   c. SW7308 Theory & Practice syllabus & bib.
   d. SW7710 Task Oriented syllabus & bib.

#20. *NEBRASKA*
   a. SW8210 Treatment Groups syllabus & bib.

#21. *UNIVERSITY NEW ENGLAND*
   a. SSW 571 SWWG syllabus
   b. SSW 571 SWWG bibliography

#22. *RUTGERS*
   a. SW 512 GW Theory & Pract. I syllabus & bib.
   b. SW 513 GW II Role Plays & Video Syllabus

#23. *TORONTO*
   a. SWK 4602 Intro. SWWG syllabus & bib.
   b. SWK 4603 Advanced SWWG: worker tech., guide for process recording
   c. SWK 4606 Non-deliberative (program) syllabus & bib.

#24. *WURZWEILER, YESHIVA*
   a. SWK 6421 SGW I Foundation syllabus
   b. SWK 6321 SGW bibliography

Index